Contents

How to use this book

Start by writing your name on the front cover – this workbook has been designed for you!

You can use it as you progress through your GCSE Religious Studies course, or as part of your revision for the final exam. It's full of different activities to help you learn by doing, not just reading.

This workbook covers both Paper 2F, which is Area of Study 2 (Judaism) and Paper 3A, which is Area of Study 3 (Philosophy and Ethics).

Activity

SB | pages 2–3

Working your way through these activities will help strengthen your understanding of some of the key topics in your GCSE course.

Follow the instructions and write your answers in the space provided.

_____

_____

_____

_____

_____

This refers to pages in this student book. You can go back to your student book to read about the topic in more depth.

There are lots of blank lines for you to write in your answers.

🔑 USEFUL TERMS

SB | pages 2–3

It's important to get to grips with some of the specialist language that we use when talking about religion. You will need to recognise these 'useful terms' because they may turn up in an exam question. And you will also need to know how to use them in your answers. These activities will help you to feel confident using religious language. Test yourself regularly on these terms.

Useful Terms Glossaries appear at the end of chapters 1, 2, 4 and 5.

Useful Terms Glossary

You can collect the meanings of useful terms here so you can refer to them at any time. You will also be creating a useful revision tool.

The (c) question in the exam asks you to 'refer to a source of wisdom and authority.' These activities will help you to memorise short quotes from religious sources, such as the Bible, and also explain what these quotes mean.

This will also be helpful for the (b) and (d) questions because you can refer to religious teachings to develop the points you make, and to back up your arguments.

TIP

Keep an eye out for these TIPS. They contain useful advice, especially to help with your exam.

EXAM PRACTICE

If you see an arrow running down the side of a box, that means the activity or activities you are doing will end with an exam practice question. These are like the questions that you will encounter in your exams. Use the information and guidance from the activities to practise these (a), (b), (c) and (d) questions.

Finally, there are two whole chapters dedicated to

Exam practice

There are four different types of question in the Edexcel exam paper – the **(a)**, **(b)**, **(c)** and **(d)** question.

Work your way through this chapter to find out what each question will look like and how it is marked.

There are some activities that will help you to understand what the examiner is looking for in an answer, and activities that practise the skills you should be demonstrating. You should then be ready to have a go at a few questions yourself.

WHAT WILL THE QUESTION LOOK LIKE?

This explains the command words that the question will use.

HOW IS IT MARKED?

This explains what the examiner will be looking for in your answer.

 REMEMBER...

This provides useful tips to help raise your marks.

All answers can be found online at **www.oxfordsecondary.co.uk/edexcel-rs-answers**, so you can mark what you've done.

Once you have filled out this workbook, you will have made your own book to revise from. That's why your name is on the cover.

Chapter 1: Judaism: Beliefs and Teachings

Activity 1.1: The Almighty

Add the statements below to the correct place in the diagram.

 pages 154–156

- Many Jews, out of respect, refer to God as Hashem, which simply means 'The Name'.

- God gave the Torah (the Law) to Moses on Mount Sinai.

- YHVH is God's holiest name. Jews believe the name of God is so holy it should not be spoken aloud.

- God has the power to rule and judge.

- Reform and Liberal Jews see this story as a metaphor, but acknowledge the universe began with God as creator.

- When Moses and the Jewish people accepted the Law, they formed a covenant (agreement) with God to keep it.

- Only God took part in Creation. Many Orthodox Jews believe everything in the universe was created by God.

- Jews daily say the Shema: 'Hashem is our God, Hashem is the one and only' (*Deuteronomy 6:4*).

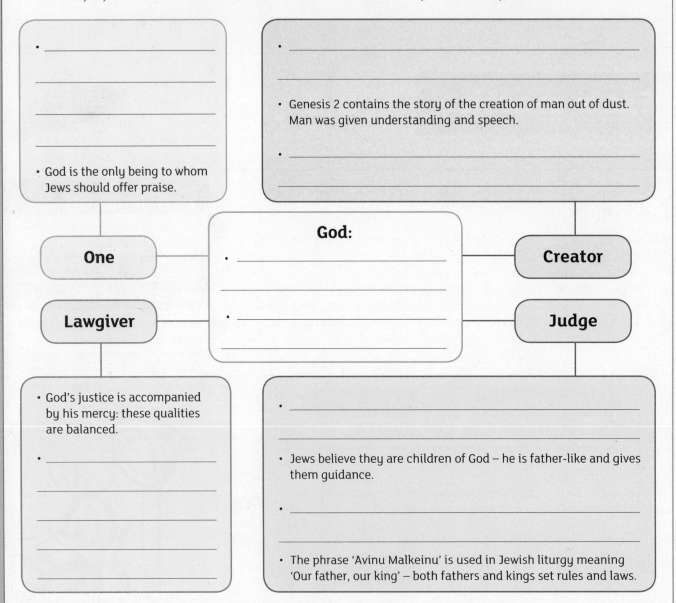

- _____
  _____
  _____
  _____
  - God is the only being to whom Jews should offer praise.

- _____
  - Genesis 2 contains the story of the creation of man out of dust. Man was given understanding and speech.
  - _____
    _____

One

Lawgiver

God:
- _____
  _____
- _____
  _____

Creator

Judge

- God's justice is accompanied by his mercy: these qualities are balanced.
- _____
  _____
  _____
  _____

- _____
  _____
- Jews believe they are children of God – he is father-like and gives them guidance.
- _____
- The phrase 'Avinu Malkeinu' is used in Jewish liturgy meaning 'Our father, our king' – both fathers and kings set rules and laws.

EXAM PRACTICE

Now answer the following exam question. Make sure you write three sentences which outline three different characteristics.

(a) Outline **three** characteristics of the Almighty shown in the Torah.   **(3 marks)**

_____

_____

_____

_____

_____

_____

_____

_____

_____

TIP

God will always be referred to as "the Almighty" in exam questions relating to Judaism.

TIP

When you're trying to answer an exam practice question, pay attention to the activities that come before it (marked by a yellow arrow). These will help to give you the correct answers.

Activity 1.2: The Shekhinah

SB   pages 157–158

Fill in the gaps in the sentences below about the Shekhinah using some of the words provided. (There are more words than gaps – you will have to decide which ones to leave out.)

| Shekhinah | synagogue | Tabernacle | Talmud |
| Tenakh | world | yeshiva | worship |

Jews believe that God continues to work in the _____.

The _____ means to 'settle or dwell' and refers to the divine presence of God in the

world. This is particularly important in relation to the study of the _____ (Hebrew

Bible) and _____ (oral or spoken laws and traditions). Studying and learning more

of God and his laws is seen as an act of _____, so the Shekhinah is present during

these activities.

As Moses was leading the Jews to the Promised Land, God told him to build a

_____, a portable temple, in which God would dwell as they travelled.

This kept the presence of God with the Jews.

USEFUL TERMS

 pages 154–158

A These terms and their meanings are muddled up. Write out the meanings in the correct order in the second table below.

Tenakh	The 'Oral Torah' – the oral laws and traditions passed down from Moses. There are two versions (Jerusalem and Babylonian)
Torah	Commandments which set rules or guide actions
Talmud	The Hebrew Bible consisting of the Torah, Nevi'im and Kethuvim
Halakhah	1) The Five Books of Moses, or 2) the written Tenakh plus the Talmud
Mitzvot	List of the 613 Mitzvot which guide Jewish life

Tenakh	
Torah	
Talmud	
Halakhah	
Mitzvot	

B Now write the correct term beside each meaning. For an extra challenge, cover up the rest of this activity and try to see if you can recall the words from memory.

The Hebrew Bible consisting of the Torah, Nevi'im and Kethuvim	
The 'Oral Torah' – the oral laws and traditions passed down from Moses. There are two versions (Jerusalem and Babylonian)	
List of the 613 Mitzvot which guide Jewish life	
Commandments which set rules or guide actions	
1) The Five Books of Moses, or 2) the written Tenakh plus the Talmud	

SOURCES OF WISDOM AND AUTHORITY

 page 159

A Learn this key quote about the Messiah.

❝Behold, days are coming […] a king will reign and prosper and he will administer justice and righteousness in the land. In his days […] Israel will dwell securely. ❞

Jeremiah 23:5–6

This quote shows how the prophet Jeremiah told the Jews a leader would come and make things right again.

Fill in the gaps below. It will help you to learn the quotation if you say the whole thing out loud every time you write it.

❝Behold, _____ are coming […] a _____ will

_____ and prosper and he will administer _____

and _____ in the land. In his days […] _____ will

_____ securely.❞

Now cover up the text above and have a go at writing out the whole quotation from memory.

❝_____

_____

_____❞

Activity 1.3: The Messiah

A Mark the following statements about belief in the Messiah as true or false.

 pages 159–160

	True	False
Messiah means 'anointed one'.	☐	☐
Messiah means 'sacred scripture'.	☐	☐
The Jewish belief in the Messiah started in the 20th century.	☐	☐
The Messiah is mentioned by the Jewish prophets.	☐	☐
The Messiah will be anointed king of Israel in the End of Days.	☐	☐
The Messiah will be a great political leader descended from King David.	☐	☐
The Messiah will ignore the Jews.	☐	☐

B Now underline which of your true answers link to the quotation from Jeremiah 23:5–6 you learned above in the Sources of Wisdom and Authority activity.

c These beginnings and endings of sentences are muddled up. Write them out correctly in the blank spaces below.

Orthodox Jews believe the Messianic Age	will be a better time of peace and harmony.
Reform and Liberal Jews believe the Messianic Age	as to when the Messiah will come.
The Messianic Age is usually referred to	means the time when the Messiah is ruling the world.
There are different beliefs	as Olam Ha-Ba.

?/ EXAM PRACTICE

Use your answers above to help you answer the following exam question.

(c) Explain **two** Jewish teachings about the Messiah. In your answer you must refer to a source of wisdom and authority. **(5 marks)**

TIP

Link your reference to a source of wisdom and authority to one of your explanations of Jewish teachings about the Messiah.

_____

_____

_____

_____

_____

Activity 1.4: The covenant at Sinai

A Tick the correct answer for each of the questions below.

SB pages 161–163

1. Who was the covenant at Sinai made with?

☐ Abraham   ☐ Isaac

☐ Moses   ☐ Jacob

2. What is the belief that God will not break his covenants called?

☐ Brit Milah   ☐ Barkhu

☐ Bar Mitzvah   ☐ Brit Olam

3. How did Moses free the Jewish people from slavery in Egypt?

☐ God sent ten plagues.

☐ God sent burning bushes.

☐ Moses enforced the Ten Commandments.

☐ Moses killed an Egyptian taskmaster.

4. Why was the covenant at Sinai different to earlier covenants?

☐ It only applied to Orthodox Jews.

☐ It applied to Jews and to people from other faiths.

☐ It said that older covenants didn't matter anymore.

☐ Any Jews who did not follow it would be punished.

5. What did God give Moses at Mount Sinai?

☐ The Torah, including the Decathlon.

☐ The Torah, including the Decadon.

☐ The Torah, including the Decalogue.

☐ The Torah, including the Decapod.

B Which of the statements below are from the Ten Commandments (Decalogue)? Tick the correct ones.

Remember the Sabbath day to sanctify it. ☐   You shall not kill. ☐

Do not sing or express joy on the Sabbath day. ☐   Consume only vegetables and fruit. ☐

You shall not recognise the gods of others in My presence. ☐   You shall attend synagogue once a week. ☐

C Answer the following question.

1. Why do you think Jews celebrate the gift of the Torah, including the Ten Commandments, every year at the festival of Shavuot? (Hint: try to include the word 'covenant' in your answer.)

> **TIP**
> You can use the Decalogue as a source of wisdom and authority in your exam.

_____

_____

Activity 1.5: The covenant with Abraham

A Write the muddled up statements from page 11 by the correct person in the family tree below.

SB pages 164–165

1. _____

_____

_____

2. _____

_____

3. _____

_____

_____

4. _____

_____

_____

5. _____

_____

1. _____

_____

2. _____

_____

3. _____

_____

Abraham — **Sarah**

Isaac — **Rebecca**

Jacob

1. _____

_____

_____

- This son was born miraculously to Abraham and Sarah.
- God called him to leave his home.
- God made a covenant with him.
- Had 12 sons who founded the tribes of Israel.
- Born approximately 1800BCE.

- God promised to found a great nation through him.
- Was nearly sacrificed by his father.
- He sealed the covenant by circumcising all the males in his family.
- Saved from sacrifice by an angel at the last minute.

B Read through Unit 7.4 in the Student Book and look at your completed family tree before answering the following questions.

TIP

There is no correct answer; what is more important is that you can explain your choice and use evidence to back it up.

1. Who do you think is more important, Moses or Abraham? Give a reason for your answer.

_____

_____

2. Choose a source of wisdom or authority you could use to support your ideas (for example, a quote or a piece of Jewish teaching).

_____

_____

Activity 1.6: The Promised Land

Fill in the gaps in the sentences below about the Promised Land using some of the words and dates provided. (There are more words than gaps – you will have to decide which ones to leave out.)

 page 165

Arabs	Promised Land		1066	Zion	British
1948	Jewish state	temple		Torah	Romans
Moses	Abraham	synagogues		Egypt	territory

The Tenakh refers to God's offer of a _____ _____ on many occasions.

This began with God's covenant with _____. Moses led the Jewish people from

_____ to Israel, the Promised Land. They were exiled from Israel by the _____

in 135CE. Jews have prayed for a return to the land, to '_____' ever since then. In the 19th century the

Zionist movement campaigned for the re-establishment of the _____ _____.

In 1947 the United Nations voted to divide the land into two states – one for the Jews and one for the

_____. In _____ CE the State of Israel was created. There have been

many disputes over this _____ since then and there is much tension because of the conflict

between Jews and Palestinians.

Prayers for the State of Israel and for the _____ government are said every Shabbat in UK

_____. Prayers for a return to Israel are also said regularly.

SOURCES OF WISDOM AND AUTHORITY

 pages 166–167

Learn these quotes about the sanctity of life.

A

'So God created Man in his Image. '
Genesis 1:27

This quotation shows that human life is holy because it comes from God.

Fill in the gaps below. It will help you to learn the quote if you say the whole thing out loud every time you write it.

'So _____ created _____ in his _____.'

Now cover up the text above and have a go at writing out the whole quotation from memory.

'_____'

B

'And a man – if he strikes mortally any human life, he shall be put to death [...] a life for a life. '
Leviticus 24:17–18

This quote shows that those who take a life are held accountable. This would have been taken literally at the time but not today.

Fill in the gaps below. It will help you to learn the quote if you say the whole thing out loud every time you write it.

'And a _____ – if he strikes _____ any human

_____, he shall be put to _____ [...] a _____ for a

_____ '

Now cover up the text above and have a go at writing out the whole quote from memory.

'_____

_____

_____'

Activity 1.7: The sanctity of life

A Re-read the quotes in the Sources of Wisdom and Authority activity opposite. Then read the following text about Pikuach Nefesh.

(SB) pages 166–168

The Talmud teaches a principle called Pikuach Nefesh, which means that keeping human life safe overrides most other laws. Talmud Yoma 83–84 gives the example of breaking the law of Shabbat to save a child from the sea or by putting out a fire.

B Now answer the following questions about these quotes and Pikuach Nefesh.

1. Why do Jews believe human life is holy?

_____

_____

2. What does Jewish law say should happen to someone who takes a life?

_____

_____

3. Why would following the principle of Pikuach Nefesh mean that doctors can answer emergency calls on Shabbat?

_____

C Mark the following statements as true or false.

	True	False
Doctors can respond to emergency calls on Shabbat.	☐	☐
Jews are permitted to hasten death if someone is in pain.	☐	☐
Even if someone is ill they have to fast on Yom Kippur.	☐	☐
The life of a pregnant mother is considered more important than that of the unborn.	☐	☐

D Now for all the statements you have marked as 'false', write one or two sentences with the correct information.

_____

_____

_____

_____

Activity 1.8: Moral principles and the Mitzvot

A These beginnings and endings of sentences are muddled up. Can you join them up correctly?

 pages 169–171

There are 613	how to perform or fulfil the Mitzvot.
The Halakhah teaches Jews	to Moses in the Torah.
Maimonides was a rabbi and one of the scholars	Mitzvot within the Torah.
Observing the Mitzvot deepens Jews' relationship	to compile the lists of Mitzvot.
Jews believe the Mitzvot were given by God	gratitude to God for rescuing them from slavery in Egypt.
Observing the Mitzvot is one way Jews show	with God.

B Now answer the following questions.

1. Below are four reasons why Jews might choose to follow the Mitzvot. Underline which you think is the strongest reason.

   • Jews believe the Mitzvot were given by God to Moses.

   • The Mitzvot are part of the covenant at Sinai.

   • The Mitzvot set out the best way to live.

   • Disobeying the Mitzvot will lead to punishment by God.

2. Explain why you think this is the strongest reason.

   _____

   _____

   _____

TIP

There is no correct or incorrect answer. What is important is that you can explain your choice and back it up with evidence.

3. Give a piece of evidence you could use to support your view. You could use a quote from the Tenakh or a Jewish teaching, for example. Think about what you have learned in other chapters, for example the covenant at Sinai.

   _____

   _____

   _____

4. Now give a reason why someone might disagree with the view you have stated above.

   _____

   _____

   _____

TIP

Look at previous units you have studied, e.g. Pikuach Nefesh in Unit 7.6.

5. Give a piece of evidence you could use to support this view.

_____

_____

_____

EXAM PRACTICE

Now answer the following exam question.

(d) 'Jews should always follow the Mitzvot.' Evaluate this statement considering arguments for and against. In your response you should:

- refer to Jewish teachings

- reach a justified conclusion. **(15 marks)**

In this question, 3 of the marks awarded will be for your spelling, punctuation and grammar and your use of specialist terminology.

> **TIP**
> Look through Units 7.6 and 7.7 in the Student Book to help you answer this question.

> **TIP**
> Remember that (d) questions relating to Jewish Beliefs and Teachings are marked out of 15 not 12, as they include an extra 3 marks for spelling, punctuation and grammar.

! REMEMBER...

- Focus your answer on the statement you are asked to evaluate.

- Try to write at least three paragraphs – one with arguments to support the statement, one with arguments to support a different point of view, and a final paragraph with a justified conclusion stating which side you think is more convincing, and why.

- Look at the bullet points in the question, and make sure you include everything that they ask for.

- The key skill that you need to demonstrate throughout your answer is **evaluation**. This means expressing judgements on whether an argument is strong or weak, based on evidence. You might decide an argument is strong because it is based on a source of religious wisdom and authority, such as a teaching from a well-known rabbi like Maimonides, or because it is something many Jews support. You might decide an argument is weak because it is based on a personal opinion, or an idea that is now outdated. You can use phrases such as 'This is a convincing argument because...' or 'In my opinion this is a weak argument because...'.

_____

_____

_____

_____

_____

_____

_____

_____
_____
_____
_____
_____
_____
_____
_____
_____
_____
_____
_____
_____
_____
_____
_____
_____
_____
_____
_____

SOURCES OF WISDOM AND AUTHORITY

page 172

Learn this quote about life after death.

A

6 Thus the dust returns to the ground, as it was, and the spirit returns to God Who gave it. 9

Ecclesiastes 12:7

There is little in the Torah about life after death. This quote comes from the Ketuvim (Writings) and suggests the soul of an individual returns to God. This could mean an afterlife with God or simply being part of him again.

Fill in the gaps below. It will help you to learn the quote if you say the whole thing out loud every time you write it.

6 Thus the _____ returns to the _____, as it was, and the

_____ returns to _____ Who gave it. 9

Now cover up the text above and have a go at writing out the whole quote from memory.

6 _____

_____ 9

Activity 1.9: Life after death

Tick the correct answer for each of the questions below.

S B pages 172–173

1. Which of the following refers to a heaven in Jewish belief?

☐ Purgatory

☐ The Garden of Eden

☐ Gan Eden

☐ Tikkun Olam

2. Which of the following is NOT a traditional belief about life after death in Judaism?

☐ Resurrection

☐ Reincarnation

☐ Those who die are gathered with their families.

☐ How you live your life does not matter – you are guaranteed to go straight to Gan Eden.

3. In Jewish belief what is Gehinnom?

☐ A place of punishment for unrighteous souls.

☐ A place of eternal rest.

☐ A place of celebration.

☐ A special synagogue.

4. What laws do gentiles (non-Jews) have to follow to be judged righteous?

☐ The Decalogue (Ten Commandments).

☐ The Seven Laws of Noah.

☐ The 613 Mitzvot.

☐ Circumcision of males.

5. Which two groups of Jews generally believe in the Messianic Age to come?

☐ Liberal and non-religious Jews

☐ Orthodox and Reform Jews

☐ Non-religious and Orthodox Jews

☐ Reform and non-religious Jews

⁇✎ EXAM PRACTICE

Now answer the following exam question.

(b) Explain **two** Jewish views on life after death. **(4 marks)**

_____

_____

_____

_____

_____

_____

_____

_____

_____

_____

_____

TIP

In your exam, a question on belief in the afterlife could ask you to compare and contrast Jewish beliefs with those of the main religious tradition of Great Britain (Christianity). This question would begin 'Describe two ....'.

Activity 1.10: Compare and contrast

In the exam question above you considered Jewish views on the afterlife. Look back at Unit 1.8 in the Student Book to refresh your understanding of Catholic views and beliefs, then answer the following question.

1. Explain **two** beliefs about the afterlife that are different between the Jewish and Catholic faiths.

1 _In Jewish belief_ _____

_____

But in Catholic belief _____

_____

2 _In Jewish belief_ _____

_____

But in Catholic belief _____

_____

Useful Terms Glossary

As you progress through the course, you can collect the meanings of useful terms in the glossary below. You can then use the completed glossaries to revise from.

To do well in the exam you will need to understand these terms and include them in your answers. Tick the shaded circles to record how confident you feel. Use the extra boxes at the end to record any other terms that you have found difficult, along with their definitions.

○ **I recognise this term**

◐ **I understand what this term means**

● **I can use this term in a sentence**

Covenant at Sinai

Abraham

Creator (as characteristic of God)

Abrahamic covenant

The Decalogue (Ten Commandments)

Afterlife

Free will

Almighty

Judge (as characteristic of God)

Covenant

Judgement

Lawgiver (as characteristic of God) _____

_____

_____

_____

One (as characteristic of God) _____

_____

_____

_____

The Messiah _____

_____

_____

_____

_____

Orthodox Jew _____

_____

_____

_____

_____

Messianic Age _____

_____

_____

_____

_____

Pikuach Nefesh _____

_____

_____

_____

_____

Mishneh Torah of Maimonides _____

_____

_____

_____

_____

The Promised Land _____

_____

_____

_____

_____

Mitzvot _____

_____

_____

_____

_____

Reform Jew _____

_____

_____

_____

_____

Moses _____

_____

_____

_____

_____

Resurrection _____

_____

_____

_____

_____

Sanctity of life _____
_____
_____
_____
_____

_____
_____
_____
_____
_____

Shekhinah _____
_____
_____
_____
_____
_____
_____

_____
_____
_____
_____
_____
_____
_____

Torah _____
_____
_____
_____
_____
_____
_____

_____
_____
_____
_____
_____
_____
_____

Chapter 2: **Judaism: Practices**

Activity 2.1: Public acts of worship

 pages 176–177

Fill in the gaps in the sentences below using some of the words provided. (There are more words than gaps – you will have to decide which ones to leave out.)

Israel	Siddur	synagogue	rabbi	Abraham
courtyards	prayer	Shabbat	Hashem	thanks
covenant	families	Temple	world	three

After the destruction of the Temple in 586BCE and again in 70CE, the most important acts of worship for

Jews were held in the _____. The most common form of worship is

_____. Prayer involves three elements: praise, _____

and making requests of God. There may be a sermon by a _____. Jews around the

_____ follow very similar services, which helps them feel connected in their faith.

Psalm 116:14–19 says, 'My vows to _____ I will pay, in the presence, now, of His

entire people […] in the _____ of the House of Hashem.' This originally referred to

the _____ in Jerusalem; for Jews today this now means the synagogue. Jews pray

towards Jerusalem in _____, the site of the Holy Temple.

Jews are expected to pray _____ times daily and there are usually synagogue services

to coincide with this. The _____ contains daily prayers used throughout the year.

On _____ there are usually services on Friday evening, and twice on Saturday.

Whole _____ are encouraged to attend synagogue on Shabbat.

Activity 2.2: The Tenakh and Talmud

Answer these questions in sentences.

 pages 178–180

1. What are the three main sections of the Tenakh?

_____

2. Where are the Torah scrolls kept in the synagogue?

_____

3. Why is the Talmud important to Jews?

_____

SOURCES OF WISDOM AND AUTHORITY

 page 179

A Learn this key quote from the Mishnah.

> ❝If a man has acquired a good name he has gained something which enriches himself; but if he has acquired words of the Torah he has attained afterlife.❞
>
> *Perkei Avot, Ch2:8*

This quote shows how highly studying the Torah is valued.

Fill in the gaps below. It will help you to learn the quote if you say the whole thing out loud every time you write it.

❝If a _____ has acquired a good _____ he has gained something

which _____ himself; but if he has acquired words of the _____

he has attained _____.❞

Now cover up the text above and have a go at writing out the whole quote from memory.

❝_____

_____

_____,❞

B Now answer the following question about this quote.

1. How does this quote show that Orthodox Jews value studying the Torah?

_____

_____

_____

Activity 2.3: Jewish food laws

A Mark the following statements about food law as true or false.

 pages 179–180

	True	False
Kashrut refers to laws about worship in the synagogue.	☐	☐
Food that is acceptable is called kosher.	☐	☐
Food that is acceptable is called treifah.	☐	☐
The food laws are originally found in the Ketuvim.	☐	☐
Pigs are treifah.	☐	☐

TIP

Learn two examples of kosher food and two examples of treifah food so you can give more detail in your exam.

	True	False
Under kosher rules, dairy and meat cannot be eaten together.	☐	☐
During the week of Passover, Jews do not eat anything that contains yeast.	☐	☐
Orthodox Jews believe the food laws are outdated and do not keep them.	☐	☐

B Now for all the statements you have marked as 'false', write a sentence with the correct information.

_____

_____

_____

_____

_____

_____

EXAM PRACTICE

Now answer the following exam question.

(b) Explain **two** ways the Talmud helps guide Jews in their everyday lives. **(4 marks)**

_____

_____

_____

_____

_____

_____

_____

_____

_____

_____

_____

_____

Activity 2.4: Private prayer

These statements about prayer in the home and private prayer are muddled up. Write them in the correct places in the table below.

 pages 181–182

- These may be carried out each day individually or as a family.
- Acknowledging God in prayer helps connect with God during the day.
- Praying before the Friday evening Shabbat meal brings the family together.
- Praying like this keeps God in an individual's heart and mind.
- This is solitary time with God.
- Jews are instructed to pray three times a day.
- After the Kiddush is recited over the wine, other blessings are made before eating the meal.
- This allows personal reflection.

> **TIP**
> In your exam, a question on practices and worship could ask you to compare and contrast Jewish practices with those of the main religious tradition of Great Britain (Christianity). Look back at Unit 2.2 in the Student Book to refresh your understanding of Catholic practices and worship when you are revising Jewish practices and worship.

Daily	Individual
•	•
•	•

Shabbat	Constant
•	•
•	•

> **TIP**
> The importance of different forms of prayer could be remembered as an acronym: DISC (Daily, Individual, Shabbat, Constant).

Activity 2.5: The Shema and Amidah

The Shema declares there is only one God. It is usually recited twice a day, in the morning and evening services in the synagogue.

 pages 183–184

A Fill in the gaps in the sentences below.

	The tallit is worn by married m_____ and some _____ over barmitzvah at every morning s_____. The fringe on the corners reminds wearers of the c_____ in the T_____.
	Tefillin are two small, black b_____ with straps worn on weekday mornings. They contain verses from the T_____. They are worn on the f_____ and a_____. This symbolically connects heart, mind and emotion to God.
	A mezuzah is a container found on the r_____ h_____ d_____ outside Jewish homes and every doorpost within that leads to a habitable room. They contain a copy of the S_____. This reminds Jews of God's p_____.

B Read the following text about the Amidah.

Amidah literally means 'standing' and refers to a series of blessings recited while standing up. It is part of the morning, afternoon and evening prayers. The Amidah consists of three sections: praise, request and thanks (except on Shabbat where the requests are left out to focus on the gift of Shabbat). Jews traditionally believe that God will respond to their prayers, although not always in the way that they expect.

C Now answer these questions in your own words.

1. What does 'Amidah' mean? _____

2. When is the Amidah recited?

_____

3. How is the Amidah used?

_____

_____

SOURCES OF WISDOM AND AUTHORITY

 page 183

A Learn this key quote from the Shema.

> ❛Hear, O Israel: Hashem is our God, Hashem is the One and Only.❜
> *Deuteronomy 6:4–5*

The Shema is the most important prayer in Judaism.

Fill in the gaps below. It will help you to learn the quote if you say the whole thing out loud every time you write it.

❛Hear, O _____: _____ is our God, _____

is the _____ and Only.❜

Now cover up the text above and have a go at writing out the whole quote from memory.

❛_____

_____❜

EXAM PRACTICE

Now answer the following exam question.

(c) Explain **two** reasons why the Shema is important. In your answer you must refer to a source of wisdom and authority.

(5 marks)

_____

_____

_____

_____

_____

_____

_____

_____

_____

_____

_____

_____

_____

_____

_____

Activity 2.6: Ritual and ceremony

Fill in the gaps in the sentences below that show differences between Orthodox and Reform or Liberal ways of celebrating particular rituals.

 pages 185–188

Ritual	Orthodox practice	Reform or Liberal practice
Birth: Naming	A girl's name is given in the synagogue when the father takes an 'aliyah' (a reading from the T_____).	There may also be a Simchat Bat which means 'R_____ for a daughter'.
Birth: Brit Milah	Boys are named during Brit Milah (ritual circumcision). This follows the covenant with A_____ who circumcised himself and his son I_____.	This might be done in hospital by a d_____ rather than a skilled circumciser.
Birth: Redemption of the firstborn Son	Pidyon ha-ben or R_____ of the Son only applies to firstborn sons born by natural birth. A small p_____ is made to a descendant of a Temple p_____.	Reform Jews generally do not follow this tradition.
Bar and Bat Mitzvah	Ceremony for boys aged 13 and girls aged 12. After this ceremony they are able to take responsibility for their own actions and f_____. After Bar Mitzvah, boys can take part in s_____ services including reading from the Torah and being part of a m_____.	Ceremony for boys and girls aged 13. After this ceremony they are able to take responsibility for their own actions and faith. Boys and g_____ can then take part in synagogue services including reading from the T_____ and being part of a minyan.
Mourning ceremonies	Many Orthodox Jews will make a t_____ in their clothes when they hear of the death of a loved one. Orthodox Jews are traditionally b_____ within 24 h_____ of death.	Reform Jews may wear a b_____ ribbon or cut a tie when they hear of the death of a loved one. Some Reform and Liberal Jews now accept c_____.

Marriage	The couple stand under a huppah symbolising a new home.	The couple stand under a
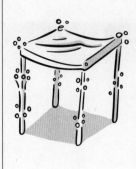	S_____ blessings are recited. At the end of the ceremony, the groom s_____ on a glass to symbolise the d_____ of the Temple. The groom gives the bride a plain metal ring. There are two religiously observant m_____ witnesses to the signing of the marriage contract (_____).	h_____ symbolising a new home. Seven blessings are recited. At the end of the ceremony, the groom stamps on a g_____ to symbolise the destruction of the T_____. The bride and groom exchange rings. Two Jewish adults, male or f_____, are witnesses to the signing of the marriage contract (ketubah). Same-sex marriage is now possible.

❓✏ EXAM PRACTICE

Now answer the following exam question.

(a) Outline **three** religious rituals Jews might take part in. **(3 marks)**

_____

_____

_____

_____

_____

_____

_____

_____

Activity 2.7: Mourning ceremonies

The following statements are muddled up. Add them in the correct order to the flowchart below, to show the ceremonies following a Jewish person's death.

 pages 187–188

- The body is washed and wrapped in a linen shroud.
- This is the complete period of mourning for all but a parent.
- The body is never left alone as a sign of respect.
- This means 'year of mourning' for a parent.
- Men are wrapped in their tallit (with tassels cut off).

- Mourners stay at home sitting on low stools or the floor.
- Mourners do not wear leather shoes, shave or cut hair, wear cosmetics or work.
- Mourners go about normal life except they do not attend parties, listen to music, shave or cut their hair.
- Anniversary day of death according to the Jewish calendar.
- Mourners pray three times daily with friends and family making up the minyan.
- Sometimes a Yahrzeit candle is lit in memory of the dead.
- Male mourners recite the Mourner's Kaddish in the synagogue.
- Plain coffins are used to show equality in death between rich and poor.

Aninut – from death to burial

-
-
-
-

Shiva – first seven days of mourning with the burial as day one

-
-
-

Sheloshim – the first thirty days of mourning with the burial as day one, including the Shiva

-
-
-

Yud-bet chodesh

-

Yahrzeit

-
-

Activity 2.8: History and celebration of Shabbat

A Read the following quote.

pages 189–191

'Between Me and the Children of Israel it is a sign forever that in a six-day period Hashem made heaven and earth, and on the seventh day He rested and was refreshed. '

Exodus 31:17

B Mark the following statements about Exodus 31:17 and how Jews celebrate Shabbat as true or false.

	True	False
Jews celebrate Shabbat to remember the covenant with Abraham.	☐	☐
Shabbat begins at dusk on Friday evening.	☐	☐
Shabbat is a time of fasting (eating no food.)	☐	☐
Jews should stay in their homes throughout Shabbat.	☐	☐
Shabbat begins with the Kiddush blessing.	☐	☐
Shabbat ends when three stars appear in the sky on Saturday evening.	☐	☐
A Shabbat service is held in the synagogue.	☐	☐

C Complete the statements in the table below about the Shabbat service in the synagogue.

Amidah	The Amidah or standing prayer is recited as the congregation face J_____
The Torah	The Torah is removed from the A_____.
Chanting the Torah	A section of the Torah is chanted by someone standing on the _____. A _____ is used to point to the words. In Orthodox synagogues it is chanted in H_____. In Reform synagogues it is also translated into E_____.
Sermon	A sermon (talk) will be given by the R_____ in the language of the congregation.
End of Shabbat service	The service finishes with p_____. The hymn A _____ O_____ is then sung.

Activity 2.9: Celebrating Shabbat today

 pages 189–191

A Read the following text about the celebration of Shabbat today.

Shabbat begins on Friday evening at dusk. This can be a challenge in the winter in countries where the light fades before the working day has finished. Some Reform Jewish communities allow their members to observe Shabbat from 6pm to help with this problem. Jews must not work during Shabbat, which includes kindling fire (*Exodus 35:3*). This means candles must be lit and food must be prepared before Shabbat begins: turning on (igniting) an oven would count as work. Orthodox Jews may also regard using a phone or driving a car as work because of the 'ignition' of the engine.

Regardless of some difficulties, Shabbat remains a time of enjoyment and a chance to connect with family. Many Jews attend synagogue services. The main Shabbat service can last about two hours and includes the Amidah or standing prayer, listening to the Torah and a sermon. The Shabbat service ends with prayers. Jews may also join Torah study groups, or meet in youth groups for discussion and social interaction.

B Now answer the following questions.

1. Explain three ways celebrating Shabbat can be a challenge in modern life.

1 _____

_____

2 _____

_____

3 _____

_____

2. Describe three religious activities that Jews may take part in during Shabbat.

1 _____

2 _____

3 _____

Activity 2.10: Festivals

A Answer the questions in the diagram below showing details of important Jewish festivals.

 pages 192–195

Rosh Hashanah (First day of Jewish New Year) September/October 	What story is remembered at Rosh Hashanah? _____ What should Jews ask of others before the judgement of God at Yom Kippur? _____ _____ What food is eaten to celebrate the New Year? _____ _____ What is blown 100 times in the synagogue? _____ What does 'Days of Awe' mean? _____

Yom Kippur (Day of Atonement) Ten days after the beginning of Rosh Hashanah	What should Jews do to prepare for Yom Kippur? _____ _____ What do many Jews do to follow the instruction in Leviticus 16 to 'deny themselves'? _____ What is the declaration Jews make at the evening service? _____ What do Jews often wear and what does it symbolise? _____ _____
Pesach (First pilgrim festival) March or April	What event recorded in the book of Exodus is remembered at Pesach or Passover? _____ _____ What food is removed completely from the home? _____ What is the most important event in Pesach? _____ Give two symbolic foods eaten at Pesach. What do they symbolise? • _____ • _____
Shavuot (Second pilgrim festival) Seven weeks after Pesach	What does this festival celebrate? _____ _____ Why might Jews take time to explore texts in a community learning programme? _____ What foods are often eaten during Shavuot? _____ Why are Pesach, Shavuot and Sukkot called the pilgrim festivals? ___ _____ _____
Sukkot (Third pilgrim festival) Four days after Yom Kippur	What is an alternative name for this festival? _____ What do Jews remember during this festival? _____ _____ Where do some Jews live during this festival? _____ _____

B Write a summary sentence for each festival explaining why it is important to Jews.

Rosh Hashanah: _____

_____

_____

Yom Kippur: _____

_____

_____

Pesach: _____

_____

Shavuot: _____

_____

_____

Sukkot: _____

_____

_____

> ## TIP
> Leviticus 23 is quite a long passage in the Torah giving instructions for different festivals which Jews should observe. Take some time to read through it. Find a short quote for each of Rosh Hashanah, Yom Kippur and Sukkot that you could use to support an explanation of why each one is important to Jews to celebrate.

EXAM PRACTICE

Now answer the following exam question.

(d) 'Festivals are the most important part of Jewish life.' Evaluate this statement considering arguments for and against. In your response you should:

- refer to Jewish teachings

- reach a justified conclusion. **(12 marks)**

> ## TIP
> You need to show 'chains of reasoning' – this means you need to link your ideas and explanations together with evidence, using phrases such as: 'this is demonstrated by' or 'this is supported by'.

! REMEMBER...

- Focus your answer on the statement you are asked to evaluate.

- Try to write at least three paragraphs – one with arguments to support the statement, one with arguments to support a different point of view, and a final paragraph with a justified conclusion stating which side you think is more convincing, and why.

- Look at the bullet points in the question, and make sure you include everything that they ask for.

- The key skill that you need to demonstrate throughout your answer is **evaluation**. This means expressing judgements on whether an argument is strong or weak, based on evidence. You might decide an argument is strong because it is based on a source of religious wisdom and authority, such as a teaching from the Talmud, or because it is something many Jews support. You might decide an argument is weak because it is based on a personal opinion, or an idea that is now outdated. You can use phrases such as 'This is a convincing argument because…' or 'In my opinion this is a weak argument because…'.

_____

_____

_____

_____

_____

_____

_____

_____

_____

_____

_____

_____

_____

Activity 2.11: Features of the synagogue

SB   **pages 196–197**

How is the synagogue used in different communities? Mark these statements as Reform tradition or Orthodox tradition.

	Most likely in Reform synagogues	Most likely in Orthodox synagogues
Often have seating on three sides facing a central bimah.	☐	☐
May be a separate balcony area for women.	☐	☐
Sometimes place the bimah at the front of the hall before the Ark.	☐	☐
Men and women sit together.	☐	☐
Men and women sit separately.	☐	☐
Married women cover their heads for modesty.	☐	☐
Both men and women are encouraged to wear the tallit and sometimes a kippah.	☐	☐
Musical instruments may be used.	☐	☐
No musical instruments are used.	☐	☐
Women can take an active part in the service.	☐	☐

USEFUL TERMS

 pages 196–197

A These terms and their meanings are muddled up. Write out the meanings in the correct order in the second table below.

Bimah	Set into the wall facing Jerusalem. It is where the Torah scrolls are kept
Yad	This is the 'eternal light' kept burning at all times in front of the Ark
Ark	The rabbi leads the service from here
Menorah	A pointer that helps the Torah to be read without touching it
Ner tamid	A seven-branched candlestick

Bimah	
Yad	
Ark	
Menorah	
Ner tamid	

B Now write the correct term beside each meaning. For an extra challenge, cover up the rest of this activity and try to see if you can recall the words from memory.

The rabbi leads the service from here	
This is the 'eternal light' kept burning at all times in front of the Ark	
A seven-branched candlestick	
Set into the wall facing Jerusalem. It is where the Torah scrolls are kept	
A pointer that helps the Torah to be read without touching it	

Useful Terms Glossary

As you progress through the course, you can collect the meanings of useful terms in the glossary below.
You can then use the completed glossaries to revise from.

To do well in the exam you will need to understand these terms and include them in your answers.
Tick the shaded circles to record how confident you feel. Use the extra boxes at the end to record any
other terms that you have found difficult, along with their definitions.

○ I recognise this term

◐ I understand what this term means

● I can use this term in a sentence

Bar Mitzvah

Amidah

Bat Mitzvah

Ark

Kashrut

Avelut

Kosher

Bimah

Liberal Jew

Brit Milah

Menorah

Mezuzah

Shavuot

Ner tamid

Sefer Torah

Pesach

Shema

Prayer

Shiva

Rosh Hashanah

Sukkot

Shabbat

Synagogue

Tallit

Yahrzeit

Talmud

Yom KIppur

Tefillin

Tenakh

Treifah

Yad

Test the (a) question

Example

1 Outline **three** ways Jews celebrate Shabbat. (3 marks)

The house is cleaned and tidied before Shabbat begins. ✔ *(1)*

The Friday night Shabbat meal is celebrated together. ✔ *(1)*

All work is avoided during Shabbat. ✔ *(1)*

! REMEMBER...

Write your answer as **three sentences**. This will help you to remember that you need to give three pieces of information. Stretch yourself to write three points and don't just repeat yourself – make each point say something new.

WHAT WILL THE QUESTION LOOK LIKE?

The (a) question will always start with the words 'Outline three...' or 'State three...', and a maximum of 3 marks will be awarded.

HOW IS IT MARKED?

In your answer you should provide three facts or short ideas; **you don't need to explain them or express any opinions.** For each correct response you will receive one mark.

Activity

2 Outline **three** beliefs about the Shekhinah. (3 marks)

The sample answer below would get only 1 mark because, although it is three accurate ideas, it is only one sentence. Rewrite the answer to gain 3 marks.

TIP

Remember, you should write three sentences to answer an 'Outline' question. Sentences start with a capital letter, end with full stop, and need to be two words or more.

Study, worship and prayer. ✔ *(1)*

_____

_____

_____

_____

_____

_____

3 Outline **three** ways Abraham showed his devotion to God. **(3 marks)**

The sample answer below (continuing on next page) would get 2 marks but it is far too long. Rewrite the first two points in shorter sentences and then add a third short point for the final mark.

Abraham was born with the name Abram around 1800BCE. He was the son of an idol maker but rejected his father's religion and believed in only one God, and is seen as the founder of Judaism. ✓ *(1)*

_____

_____

God called Abraham to leave his home and family, which he did, and as a result he would be rewarded with many descendants and a great land, which is still important to Jews today. ✓ *(1)*

_____

_____

_____

_____

4 Outline **three** forms of Jewish prayer. **(3 marks)**

_____

_____

_____

_____

_____

_____

5 Outline **three** features of Jewish mourning ceremonies. **(3 marks)**

_____

_____

_____

_____

_____

_____

Test the (b) question

Example

1 Explain **two** Jewish beliefs about the Messianic Age. **(4 marks)**

Firstly, for most Orthodox Jews, the Messianic Age means the time when the Messiah has arrived and is ruling the world. ✓ **(1)** *It is called Olam Ha-Ba.* ✓ **(1)**

Secondly, for many Reform Jews, the Messianic Age will be a time of peace and harmony. ✓ **(1)** *This will be achieved through the good deeds of Jews.* ✓ **(1)**

> **! REMEMBER...**
>
> Make **two different points**. Try to show the examiner where each point begins. For example, start your answer with 'Firstly...' and then move on to your second point by saying 'Secondly...'.
>
> Try to **develop** each point with an example or more explanation. Developing your points will earn you more marks.

WHAT WILL THE QUESTION LOOK LIKE?

The (b) question will always start with the words '**Explain two...**' or '**Describe two...**', and a maximum of **4 marks** will be awarded. You are asked to 'Explain' or 'Describe', which means you will need to show **development** of ideas.

HOW IS IT MARKED?

This answer would gain 4 marks because it makes two different points, and both points are clearly developed.

Activity

2 Explain **two** ways in which the principle of Pikuach Nefesh could be applied to Jews today. **(4 marks)**

The sample answer below would get 2 marks because it makes one point and then develops it with more explanation. Add a second point for 1 more mark. If you can develop that point with an appropriate example or more explanation, you will get the total 4 marks available.

A first example would be a doctor could answer an emergency call during Shabbat. ✓ **(1)** *Saving a life is supremely important to Jews and a life or death situation would clearly be responded to.* ✓ **(1)**

A second example could be _____

_____

_____

_____

_____

TIP

Remember that to develop a point you need to give an example or more explanation. Phrases such as 'This means that...', 'This is where...', or 'For example...' can be a good way to start developing a point.

3 Explain **two** reasons why worshipping in public is important to Jews today. **(4 marks)**

The sample answer below would get 2 out of 4 marks as neither point is developed. Develop each point fully for a maximum of 2 additional marks.

One reason is that it reminds Jews that they are part of a community. ✓ **(1)**

_____

_____

_____

A second reason is to praise God. ✓ **(1)**

_____

_____

_____

TIP

You need to understand Jewish traditions from a historical point of view, but you will often be asked to think about how Jews practise their faith today. This means considering how modern life can affect traditions and understanding.

4 Explain **two** features of the Shabbat meal. **(4 marks)**

This student had got confused. Which point would you remove from the sample answer below? Replace it with another developed point that does relate to the Shabbat meal.

After seeking forgiveness from others, they ask forgiveness from God, who then finalises his judgement and decides their fate for the year ahead.

The meal is celebrated with family and special Shabbat hymns are sung.

_____

_____

_____

_____

_____

TIP

What has the student got muddled with Shabbat?

5 Explain **two** features of Jewish birth ceremonies. **(4 marks)**

_____

_____

_____

_____

_____

_____

_____

_____

6 Describe **two** differences in worship between Judaism and the main religious tradition of Great Britain. **(4 marks)**

_____

_____

_____

_____

_____

_____

_____

TIP

Compare and contrast questions are rare but they will ask you to compare Jewish beliefs with those of the main religious tradition of Great Britain, which is Christianity. They will only ask you to compare **either** belief in the afterlife, or practices and worship. Make sure you look at the Catholic unit 1.8 when you revise the Jewish unit 7.8, and the Catholic unit 2.2 when you revise the Jewish unit 8.4 to help you understand the differences between the two faiths.

Test the (c) question

Example

1 | Explain **two** characteristics of the Almighty that are shown in the Torah. In your answer you must refer to a source of wisdom and authority. **(5 marks)**

The first characteristic is that of the Creator. ✓ **(1)** *Jews believe that no other being took part in Creation, and everything in the universe was created by Hashem.* ✓ **(1)** *This is made clear in Genesis when it says, 'Hashem formed the man of dust from the ground, and He blew into his nostrils the soul of life'.* ✓ **(1)**

The second characteristic is of Lawgiver. ✓ **(1)** *Jews see the Torah as a gift; given to Moses on Mount Sinai. This enables them to lead good lives and please Hashem.* ✓ **(1)**

! REMEMBER...

The 5 mark question is similar to the 4 mark question, so try to make **two different points** and **develop** each of them.

The additional instruction in the question asks you to **'refer to a source of wisdom and authority'**. Try to think of a reference to the Tenakh, Talmud, a prayer or a quote from a rabbi or scholar that can back up one of your points. You only need one reference.

WHAT WILL THE QUESTION LOOK LIKE?

The (c) question will always start with the words **'Explain two...'** and end with the words **'In your answer you must refer to a source of wisdom and authority'**. A maximum of **5 marks** will be awarded.

HOW IS IT MARKED?

This answer would gain 5 marks because it makes two different points, and both points are clearly developed. It also refers to a relevant source of wisdom and authority.

Activity

2 | Explain **two** reasons why Rosh Hashanah is important to Jews. In your answer you must refer to a source of wisdom and authority. **(5 marks)**

The key source of wisdom and authority for Rosh Hashanah is: 'in the seventh month, on the first of the month there shall be a rest day for you' *(Leviticus 23:24, RSV-CE)*. Develop a point around this quote, then add a second separate point explaining why Rosh Hashanah is important.

_____

_____

_____

_____

_____

_____

_____

_____

_____

_____

3 Explain **two** Jewish beliefs about life after death. In your answer you must refer to a source of wisdom and authority. **(5 marks)**

The sample answer below contains one point with far too much information, and one with too little. Rewrite and shorten the first point, making sure it would still get 3 marks. Develop the second point to make it worth 2 marks.

The first belief that some Jews hold is that a Jew will return to God, therefore there is an afterlife even if they don't know what it will be like. ✓ **(1)** This is made clear in Ecclesiastes when it says, 'the spirit returns to God who gave it'. ✓ **(1)** This is one of the few occasions that life after death is mentioned in the Torah. As such, Jews do not all believe the same thing about life after death. ✓ **(1)**

The second belief is in Gad Eden. ✓ **(1)**

> **TIP**
>
> Remember you don't need to put the full reference – if you do put the reference and it is wrong, you will lose any credit, even if the quote is correct.

_____

_____

_____

_____

_____

_____

_____

_____

_____

_____

4 Explain **two** features of public worship for Jews. In your answer you must refer to a source of wisdom and authority. **(5 marks)**

Three prompts are given below. Use them to write a complete answer to this question. You will need to develop both the points and link one of them to the source of wisdom and authority to gain full marks.

'My vows to Hashem I will pay, in ... the House of Hashem' (Psalm 116:14–19)

Shabbat services

Daily prayers

_____

_____

_____

_____

_____

_____

_____

_____

_____

5 Explain **two** reasons why the covenant at Sinai is important to Jews. In your answer you
must refer to a source of wisdom and authority. **(5 marks)**

_____

_____

_____

_____

_____

_____

_____

_____

_____

Test the (d) question

Example

1 'Jews must keep all laws in the Torah.'

Evaluate this statement considering arguments for and against. In your response you should:

- refer to Jewish teachings

- reach a justified conclusion. **(15 marks)**

In this question, 3 of the marks awarded will be for your spelling, punctuation and grammar and your use of specialist terminology.

WHAT WILL THE QUESTION LOOK LIKE?

The (d) question will always ask you to **evaluate** a statement. The bullet points underneath will tell you the things the examiner expects to see in your answer. Here, it says you need to 'refer to Jewish teachings', so make sure you write about core Jewish beliefs, or important sources of Jewish wisdom and authority. The final bullet will always ask you to 'reach a justified conclusion'.

SPaG

On Paper 2F, you will be assessed on the quality of your written communication in question 1 (d) – relating to Jewish Beliefs and Teachings. A maximum of 3 marks will be awarded for consistent accuracy in your **spelling, punctuation and grammar**, and for using a wide range of specialist terms. Allow yourself time in the exam to check this (d) answer carefully.

! REMEMBER...

To evaluate the statement, you need to:
- explain why some people might agree with the statement
- give reasons, including Jewish views
- say whether you think this is a strong or weak argument, and explain why.

Then:
- explain why other people might disagree with the statement
- give reasons, including Jewish views
- say whether you think this is a strong or weak argument, and explain why.

What might make a strong argument?
- Based on a religious source of wisdom and authority, for example a teaching from the Talmud, or from a rabbi.

What might make a weak argument?
- Based on personal opinion rather than a religious teaching.
- A popular idea with no supporting evidence.

Reaching a justified conclusion means you need to:
- explain which side of the argument you think has the strongest evidence
- refer to this evidence briefly.

HOW IS IT MARKED?

The examiner will mark your answer using a mark scheme based on level descriptors, similar to the ones below.

Level descriptors

Level 1 (1–3 marks)	• Basic information or issues related to the topic are loosely identified and can be explained with limited religious or moral understanding.
	• Judgements are given but not fully explained or justified.
Level 2 (4–6 marks)	• Some information or issues related to the topic are identified and can be explained with religious or moral understanding.
	• Judgements are given with some attempt to appraise the evidence, but they are not fully explained or justified.
Level 3 (7–9 marks)	• Information given clearly describes religious information/issues, leading to coherent and logical chains of reasoning that consider different viewpoints. These are supported by an accurate understanding of religion and belief.
	• The answer contains coherent and reasoned judgements of many, but not all, of the elements in the question. Judgements are supported by a good understanding of evidence, leading to a partially justified conclusion.

Level 4 (10–12 marks)	• The response critically deconstructs religious information/issues, leading to coherent and logical chains of reasoning that consider different viewpoints. These are supported by a sustained, accurate and thorough understanding of religion and belief.
	• The answer contains coherent and reasoned judgements of the full range of elements in the question. Judgements are fully supported by the comprehensive use of evidence, leading to a fully justified conclusion.

Here are four sample answers to the question on the previous page. Each one would be awarded a different level. Read through the answers to get an idea of what a level 1, 2, 3 or 4 answer looks like.

Level 1 sample answer:

This is a Level 1 answer because:
- it only gives brief reasons to support one side of the argument
- there is very little evaluation of the arguments.

To improve this answer the student should:
- include the other side of the argument plus reasons to support it
- explain whether they think the arguments are strong or weak.

Jews cannot keep all the laws in the Torah as they were written a long time ago and things are different in the modern world.

Rabbis will help Jews decide which laws are important to keep today, but the Ten Commandments are considered important and should be kept.

Overall, most Jews wouldn't agree with the statement as there are too many.

TIP
Make sure you use the Jewish names for their holy writings such as Torah or Tanakh.

TIP
Remember there are lots of different groups of Jews – linking a belief to a specific group will always improve your answer.

Level 2 sample answer:

This is a Level 2 answer because:
- it refers to different arguments linked to the statement
- it comes to a conclusion about which side is correct.

To improve this answer the student should:
- evaluate how strong or weak each of the arguments is
- explain why they think the arguments are strong or weak.

Despite the Mitzvot (laws) being important to Jews because they were given to Moses as part of the covenant, they were written a long time ago and it is near impossible to keep all 613 laws today when some need a Temple, for example.

Rabbis will help Jews decide which laws are important to still keep today. The Ten Commandments are often seen as the most important as they were given first, therefore they should always be kept.

However, Orthodox Jews do aim to keep as many of the laws as they can as they believe they are a blessing from God to lead their lives. This backs up the statement as to come from God means they must be kept.

I think most Jews though would see this argument as incorrect and also say that the laws are outdated nowadays, therefore I disagree with the statement. There is no point keeping outdated laws.

TIP
Factual information is useful in answers to (d) questions, but remember, don't just list lots of facts – evaluate each one!

TIP
Clear paragraphs always help structure an answer. The word 'However' is a clear indication of the second point of view in this answer.

Level 3 sample answer:

This is a Level 3 answer because:
- it evaluates arguments on both sides
- it comes to a conclusion based on this evaluation.

To improve this answer the student should:
- give some more evidence on each side to strengthen the arguments
- evaluate this evidence.

Despite the Mitzvot (laws) being important to Jews because they were given to Moses as part of the Torah, they were written a long time ago and it is near impossible to keep all 613 laws today because there is no Temple for those ones that need it and laws in countries outside Israel are different. It does highlight their importance in Jewish life, as they were given to Moses by Hashem. Additionally, Jews still regard Moses as a great teacher in Judaism. This makes the argument that the laws he was given by God are important to follow convincing for many Jews.

Additionally, rabbis continue to study and help Jews decide which laws are still important to keep today. So it is clear that even the teachers in Judaism do not feel it is possible to follow every law as they were originally written. For example, Mitzvot related to Shabbat need to be interpreted for modern living. The Ten Commandments are often still seen as the most important as they were given first, with the first commandment making clear that there is just one God who saved the Jewish people. Therefore it is important Jews continue to follow these, and most Jews would agree with this.

However, Orthodox Jews do aim to keep as many of the laws as they can as they believe they are a blessing from God to lead their lives, although some Mitzvot such as those regarding temple sacrifice are naturally not followed. This is a strong reason as Jews believe that following the Mitzvot, or not, determines Olam Ha-Ba, 'The world to come'.

However, overall, I find the arguments from Reform Jews more convincing. Due to their age, it is a strong argument to claim that the Mitzvot need reinterpreting and to be selectively followed if Jews are to live a sensible life in the modern world.

> ### TIP
> To reach Level 3 you should evaluate the arguments for each side. Don't just wait until you get to the conclusion. Using phrases such as 'This makes the argument ... convincing' is a good way to show that you are evaluating.

> ### TIP
> Make sure you write a justified conclusion, rather than just giving your personal opinion. This conclusion is 'justified' because it refers to the evidence that has led the student to agree with the statement.

Level 4 sample answer:

This is a Level 4 answer because:
- there is a clear line of argument throughout
- it evaluates the arguments it presents and leads to a clear conclusion
- there is evidence the student knows a lot about the topic, and the whole answer is clearly linked to the statement.

The Mitzvot (laws) were given to Moses as part of the covenant on Mount Sinai and so are very important to Jews today. However, they were recorded a long time ago and this is important because modern life is very different. Many Jews do not live in Israel, which has agricultural laws to follow Mitzvot and there is no Temple, which some Mitzvot refer to. It is near impossible to keep all 613 laws today when we live in such a different way.

However, their appearance in the Torah does highlight the reason for the laws' importance in Jewish life: they were given to Moses by Hashem. Additionally, Jews still regard Moses as instrumental in the Jews being identified as the chosen people of God, making arguments that his laws should be kept, very convincing for many Jews. The Torah is the Jewish holy book, and as such Orthodox Jews would argue its laws must be kept in obedience to God and to fulfil the covenant Moses made with him at Sinai.

With the presence of the Shekhinah and the Talmud, rabbis continue to study the Mitzvot to help Jews decide which laws are still important to keep today. For example, Mitzvot related to Shabbat need to be interpreted for modern living; this means they are not all followed, but understood in a modern context. The Ten Commandments are seen as the most important laws as they were given to Moses first. The first commandment states that there is just one God who saved the Jewish people, which adds weight to the argument of Orthodox Jews that it is important to keep all the laws he gave. Most Jews would agree they are expected to follow these ten Mitzvot.

Yet Orthodox Jews keep as many others as they can, believing the Mitzvot to be a 'blessing' from God (Deuteronomy 11:26). However, even they must make some adjustments: temple sacrifice for example is not followed. Many feel following the laws in the Torah – or not – is crucial as it will determine Olam Ha-Ba, 'The world to come'. Despite this view in traditional Judaism, some Jews in the Reform or Liberal branches of Judaism prefer to keep the Ten Commandments and only as many of the other Mitzvot that can be incorporated into modern life, as they feel this argument is not convincing.

Overall, given the adjustments all groups of Judaism choose to make, and sometimes have to make, it would seem it is impossible in the modern world to keep all the laws in the Torah. The Mitzvot were written in the context of an ancient society and it seems they need reinterpreting and modern Jews should follow them selectively. Trying to keep as many as you are able still allows Jews to be faithful to God.

TIP

Additional detail here about how the rabbis interpret the Mitzvot shows the breadth of the student's knowledge. This makes the argument being made much stronger.

TIP

Ensure you start a new paragraph when beginning a divergent (different) view. It is also helpful to start with a phrase such as 'Yet...', 'However...' or 'On the other hand...'.

TIP

Accurate sources of wisdom and authority can be useful for providing evidence to back up your arguments in the (d) question.

Activity

2 'The Promised Land is the most significant part of the covenant with Abraham.'

Evaluate this statement considering arguments for and against. In your response you should:

- refer to Jewish teachings
- reach a justified conclusion. **(15 marks)**

In this question, 3 of the marks awarded will be for your spelling, punctuation and grammar and your use of specialist terminology.

A Read the sample answer below.

For many Jews, the land of Israel remains a high priority indicating the strength of the above claim. It is central to the history of the faith and represents the promise that Hashem made to his people. A further indication of its importance are the prayers for a return to the Promised Land on Shabbat and at the end of the Passover saying, 'Next year in Jerusalem!' These references present a convincing argument to suggest that the idea of the Promised Land, and in fact a return to it, are the most significant part of the covenant and high priority for Jews.

However, other Jews may see that the promise of offspring, and being the father to a great nation is clearly more significant. Without people, there would be no land needed. Jews may also not agree with the need to have a physical Promised Land as the politics of Israel are complicated, and Jews are now settled around the world. This seems to quite significantly undermine some of the other arguments.

Alternatively, other Jews may see the sealing of the covenant by circumcising as important, as Jews still continue this practice today. Yet, it seems more like an outward sign rather than a fundamental part like the idea of being a great nation or living in a Promised Land.

After considering different views, it seems clear that the most convincing argument is that the people of the 'great nation' are more significant than the land to live in, or the signs such as circumcision. Without the people, now known as the Jews, everything else would simply be history.

B Now answer the following questions about the sample answer above.

1. The student makes two main points in their supporting argument. What are they?

_____

_____

_____

2. Do you agree that this is a strong argument? Why or why not?

_____

_____

_____

3. The student gives two other possible points of view. What are they?

_____

_____

_____

4. Which of the three points of view does the student suggest is most convincing? Why?

_____

_____

_____

5. Do you agree with the student's final conclusion? Why or why not?

_____

_____

_____

6. The question says you should 'refer to Jewish teachings'. Using a coloured pen, highlight any references to Jewish teaching that you can find.

7. The question also asks you to 'reach a justified conclusion'. Circle the sentence where the student gives their judgement. Then underline the sentence where they summarise their evidence.

8. Can you find and highlight any phrases which show that the student is evaluating the arguments?

TIP

Remember, evaluating means making a judgement about how strong or weak an argument is, based on evidence.

3 'The most essential quality of the Almighty is being a creator.'

Evaluate this statement considering arguments for and against. In your response you should:

- refer to Jewish teachings

- reach a justified conclusion.   **(15 marks)**

In this question, 3 of the marks awarded will be for your spelling, punctuation and grammar and your use of specialist terminology.

Here is the beginning of a response to the question above, which gives some arguments in support of the statement. To complete the answer you need to give arguments against the statement and a justified conclusion.

To move above Level 2 you also need to include judgements, evaluating how convincing you find the arguments to be.

Complete the answer below.
- Begin your first paragraph with the sentence, 'However some Jews would disagree with these ideas because...'
- Include arguments from different Jewish points of view which many support or oppose your arguments.
- Include some evaluation, such as 'This argument is strong/weak because...'
- Finally, add a justified conclusion. This could begin, 'After considering both sides of the argument, the most convincing reason is...'

Many Jews would find this argument convincing as the Torah begins with Hashem creating the universe. It is a core Jewish belief that the Almighty created the world which makes this a strong argument and hard to overcome. Even the different groups of Jews who may disagree about how literally to take the story, would all agree that the Almighty was the creator, adding further strength to the argument.

_____

_____

_____

_____

_____

_____

_____

_____

_____

_____

_____

_____

TIP

Remember there are four different characteristics to consider: One, Creator, Lawgiver and Judge.

4 'Belief in life after death is important to Jews.'

Evaluate this statement considering arguments for and against. In your response you should:

- refer to Jewish teachings
- reach a justified conclusion. **(15 marks)**

In this question, 3 of the marks awarded will be for your spelling, punctuation and grammar and your use of specialist terminology.

Read the sample answer below. This is a Level 1 answer. To attain a higher level you need to:

- include evaluation, which means expressing whether you think an argument is convincing or not, and explaining why you think this
- use chains of reasoning in your arguments
- add a justified conclusion.

Rewrite the answer below to include these things.

- Evaluate each argument as you go along – don't wait until the conclusion.
- Use phrases such as 'This argument is strong/weak because…'
- Reach your own conclusion. You don't have to agree with the statement; the important thing is to say why you agree or disagree.

Life after death, as for most human beings, is an important consideration for Jews. They would focus on following the Mitzvot in order to reach Gan Eden and avoid Gehinnom. They want to avoid the punishment that is warned of in Exodus.

Other Jews would simply not worry about life after death and focus on their life now. As such, the most important thing for them would be to follow the Mitzvot and please Hashem. This is as there is so little about it in the Torah.

5 'Festivals remain important for Jews today.'

Evaluate this statement considering arguments for and against. In your response you should:

- refer to Jewish teachings
- reach a justified conclusion. **(12 marks)**

> **! REMEMBER...**
>
> - Focus your answer on the statement you are asked to evaluate.
> - Try to write at least three paragraphs – one with arguments to support the statement, one with arguments to support a different point of view, and a final paragraph with a justified conclusion stating which side you think is more convincing, and why.
> - Look at the bullet points in the question, and make sure you include everything that they ask for.
> - The key skill that you need to demonstrate throughout your answer is **evaluation**. This means expressing judgements on whether an argument is strong or weak, based on evidence. You might decide an argument is strong because it is based on a source of religious wisdom and authority, such as a teaching from the Talmud, or because it is something many Jews support. You might decide an argument is weak because it is based on a personal opinion, or an idea that is now outdated. You can use phrases such as 'This is a convincing argument because…' or 'In my opinion this is a weak argument because…'.

Chapter 4: Philosophy and Ethics: Arguments for the Existence of God

Activity 4.1: Revelation

A These beginnings and endings of sentences are muddled up. Write them out correctly in the blank spaces below.

SB pages 202–203

Revelation means	God is communicating and teaching.
Catholics use revelation to mean	revelation is proof of God's existence.
God is not trying to prove he exists:	to uncover something previously hidden.
However, Christians may believe that	how God makes himself known to humans.

B Fill in the gaps in the diagram below using some of the words provided. (There are more words than gaps – you will have to decide which ones to leave out.)

God   Holy Spirit   Bible   revealed   revelation   miracles   Jesus   Church

God first _____ himself
to people like Moses in the Old Testament.

Catholics believe that today, through
the _____ and the
_____ _____,
people can encounter Jesus and
therefore God.

Jesus

Catholics believe Jesus is the
final _____; he was
_____ in human form.

_____ is proof to Christians
of the existence of God.

EXAM PRACTICE

Now answer the following exam question.

(a) Outline **three** things that the revelation of Jesus shows about God. **(3 marks)**

_____

_____

_____

_____

_____

_____

_____

TIP

Think love, sacrifice and sacrifice! But remember you need to make these into three separate sentences.

Activity 4.2: Visions

Ⓐ Read the text below about why visions may or may not lead people to believe in God. | (SB) **pages 204–205**

Visions may be seen as a type of private revelation, but are only accepted by Catholics if they do not contradict the teaching of the Church. Visions take many forms:

- Corporeal visions: physically seeing something
- Imaginative visions: seeing something in dreams.

Visions can be powerful personal experiences giving strength and faith to those who experience them. However, others argue that there is no lasting or physical proof of visions: they could be hallucinations, misunderstandings or just made up.

Catholics maintain that there are many examples in the Bible and history. It has been suggested that if God exists, we would expect him to make contact. However, even if a vision is genuine, not everyone agrees that this is then proof of God. Dreams could be wish fulfilment, for example: a subconscious desire to have a religious experience.

Ⓑ Now fill in the table below with reasons for against visions as proof that God exists.

Reasons why visions might lead people to believe in God	Reasons against visions as proof that God exists

c These statements about visions are muddled up. Write them in the correct places in the table below.

- Joan of Arc had visions of several saints and as a result tried to force the English from her homeland of France.

- The voice of God said, 'This is my beloved Son, with whom I am well pleased; listen to him' (*Matthew 17:5, RSV-CE*).

- Abraham was visited by God with a promise of protection and reward (*Genesis 15*).

- During the transfiguration of Jesus, Moses and Elias appeared to Jesus, Peter, James and John.

- She was later captured by the English and burnt at the stake.

- 'Fear not, Abram, I am your shield; your reward shall be very great' (*Genesis 15:1, RSV-CE*).

Bible: Old Testament	•
	•
Bible: New Testament	•
	•
Non-biblical	•
	•

EXAM PRACTICE

Now answer the following exam question.

(d) 'A Catholic should see visions as proof that God exists.' Evaluate this statement considering arguments for and against. In your response you should:

· refer to Catholic teachings

· refer to different Christian points of view

· reach a justified conclusion. **(15 marks)**

In this question, 3 of the marks awarded will be for your spelling, punctuation and grammar and your use of specialist terminology.

TIP

Catholic teachings for this question could include examples of visions from the Old Testament, New Testament or the saints.

 REMEMBER...

· Focus your answer on the statement you are asked to evaluate.

· Try to write at least three paragraphs – one with arguments to support the statement, one with arguments to support a different point of view, and a final paragraph with a justified conclusion stating which side you think is more convincing, and why.

· Look at the bullet points in the question, and make sure you include everything that they ask for.

· The key skill that you need to demonstrate is **evaluation**. This means expressing judgements on whether an argument is strong or weak, based on evidence. You might decide an argument is strong because it is based on a source of religious wisdom and authority, such as a teaching from the Bible, or because it is based on scientific evidence. You might decide an argument is weak because it is based on a personal opinion, or a popular idea with no scientific basis. You can use phrases such as 'This a convincing argument because…' or 'In my opinion this is a weak argument because…'.

Activity 4.3: Miracles

Miracles are things that appear to break the laws of nature. Catholics and other Christians claim the only explanation can be God. They have been recorded throughout history and may lead a person to faith or strengthen existing faith.

 **pages 206–208**

A Answer the following questions.

Biblical examples of miracles:	Non-biblical examples of miracles
1. Who parted and crossed the Red Sea?	**1.** Who appeared to Juan Diego in Mexico?
2. At what event did Jesus turn water into wine?	**2.** What is unusual about the image in Guadalupe?
3. What did Jesus do at Beth-Sa'ida?	**3.** Who did the Virgin Mary appear to in Lourdes?
4. What was unusual about Jesus' healing of the official's son?	**4.** What kind of miracles have happened at Lourdes since?

B For each statement tick the correct column.

	A reason why miracles might lead people to believe in God	An argument against miracles as proof of God
Coincidences of unusual/uncommon events do occur.	☐	☐
Those who experience them feel like they have had direct contact with God.	☐	☐
No natural scientific explanation means that only God is a possible explanation.	☐	☐
Scientific and medical knowledge is continuing to develop.	☐	☐
Inexplicable things do not necessarily mean the answer is God.	☐	☐
Natural laws have been broken.	☐	☐

QUE SOY ERA IMMACULADA COUNCEPCIOU

USEFUL TERMS

 pages 209–211

A These terms and their meanings are muddled up. Write out the meanings in the correct order in the second table below.

Faith	A person or thing who brings something into existence
Omnipotence	Having a mysterious, spiritual or holy quality
Creator	The belief that God is all powerful
Numinous	Going beyond human experience and existing outside the physical world
Transcendent	Strong spiritual belief

Faith	
Omnipotence	
Creator	
Numinous	
Transcendent	

B Now write the correct term beside each meaning. For an extra challenge, cover up the rest of this activity and try to see if you can recall the words from memory.

The belief that God is all powerful	
Going beyond human experience and existing outside the physical world	
Having a mysterious, spiritual or holy quality	
A person or thing who brings something into existence	
Strong spiritual belief	

SOURCES OF WISDOM AND AUTHORITY

 pages 209–211

Learn some quotations about revelation from the Catechism of the Catholic Church.

A

‘Yet even if Revelation is already complete, it has not been made completely explicit; it remains for Christian faith gradually to grasp its full significance’
Catechism of the Catholic Church 66

This quote shows that although Catholics believe that Jesus was the final and complete revelation, there is more to learn and understand about his revelation.

Fill in the gaps below. It will help you to learn the quote if you say the whole thing out loud every time you write it.

‘Yet even if _____ is already complete, it has not been made completely

_____; it remains for _____ faith gradually to grasp its full

_____ ’

Now cover up the text above and have a go at writing out the whole quote from memory.

‘_____

_____

_____ ’

B

‘Throughout the ages, there have been so-called ‘private’ revelations, some of which have been recognised by the authority of the Church. They do not belong, however, to the deposit of faith.’
Catechism of the Catholic Church 67

This quote shows that religious experiences can provide insights into God, but will not contain any new information.

Fill in the gaps below. It will help you to learn the quote if you say the whole thing out loud every time you write it.

‘Throughout the _____, there have been so-called ‘_____’

revelations, some of which have been _____ by the _____ of the

Church. They do not _____, however, to the _____ of faith. ’

Now cover up the text above and have a go at writing out the whole quote from memory.

‘_____

_____

_____ ’

C

'Christian faith cannot accept 'revelations' that claim to surpass or correct the Revelation of which Christ is the fulfilment'

Catechism of the Catholic Church 67

This quote shows that any religious experience recognised as authentic will always be less important than the revelation of Jesus and can only help to understand what has already been revealed.

Fill in the gaps below. It will help you to learn the quote if you say the whole thing out loud every time you write it.

'Christian _____ cannot accept '_____' that claim

to _____ or correct the Revelation of which _____ is the

_____'

Now cover up the text above and have a go at writing out the whole quote from memory.

'_____

_____

_____

_____

_____'

Activity 4.4: Religious experiences and the question of proof

Write a sentence in the right hand column to explain each argument against the idea that religious experiences are proof that God exists. One has been done for you.

 pages 209–211

Why religious experiences may not be proof that God exists	Explanation
Laws of nature	The laws of nature are unbreakable and everyone experiences this every day. Miracles contradict the laws of nature, but only a few people experience them. Therefore it would be more reasonable to trust the laws of nature than to trust that a miracle has happened.
Lack of evidence	

Use of stimulants	
Hallucinations	
Wish fulfilment	

?/ **EXAM PRACTICE**

Now answer the following exam question.

(b) Explain **two** reasons why Catholics might use religious experiences as an argument for the existence of God.

(4 marks)

_____

_____

_____

_____

_____

_____

_____

_____

_____

_____

_____

TIP

Remember you need two totally different reasons in the (b) question. Avoid saying similar things in each point. Use 'firstly' and then 'secondly', making sure you start each point on a new line.

Activity 4.5: The design argument

The design argument can be summarised as follows:

1. There appears to be design in the world.

2. If there is design, it implies a designer.

3. This designer is God.

pages 212–213

TIP

Remember the design argument is also called the teleological argument (teleology = the study of design / purpose).

A Look at the following images and write down what each one has to do with the design argument.

William Paley

_____

_____

_____

Thomas Aquinas

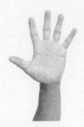

_____

_____

_____

The eye and a camera

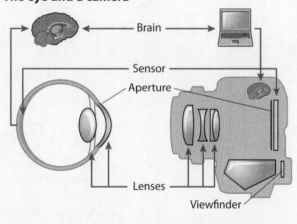

_____

_____

_____

_____

B Complete the sentences below to explain why the design argument is a strong argument. Each one has been started, but you need to make them into developed points.

1. It is based on our own experience; many things in nature _____

_____

_____

2. It completes a Christian view of the nature of God, an _____ and _____ God

is able to _____

_____

c What is the evidence against the design argument? How would Catholics respond to these arguments? Complete the table below with the missing evidence and Catholic responses.

Evidence against the design argument	Catholic responses
Hume said the universe is unique – we can't use analogies to explain it.	
	Humans can learn from suffering and evil – and some is caused by free will.
	Science supports the idea of order.
Evolution is an explanation of order and purpose.	

Activity 4.6: The cosmological argument

The cosmological argument can be summarised as follows:

1. There is cause and effect in the world.

2. There needs to be a first cause.

3. This can only be God.

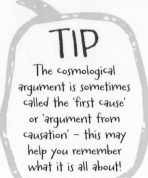

TIP

The cosmological argument is sometimes called the 'first cause' or 'argument from causation' – this may help you remember what it is all about!

$$\boxed{SB}$$ pages 214–215

A Fill in the gaps in the sentences below about the strengths of the cosmological argument using some of the words provided. (There are more words than gaps – you will have to decide which ones to leave out.)

| Bang | effect | scientific | cause |
| illogical | regress | law | logical |

It is based on the _____ of cause and _____ .

It is more _____ than the alternative – infinite

_____ . It is compatible with _____ evidence,

such as the Big _____ .

TIP

Don't get the design and cosmological arguments confused! It is easy to mix them up, but this will lose you marks!

B What is the evidence against the cosmological argument? How would Catholics respond to these arguments? Complete the table below with the missing evidence and Catholic responses.

Evidence against the cosmological argument	Catholic responses
Russell suggests that a total explanation is impossible.	
	If all things in the universe can have their cause investigated, why can't the universe itself?
The first cause does not need to be God.	

Activity 4.7: The existence of suffering

Evil in the world creates a potential problem for religious believers. Catholics believe evil can be a consequence of free will. Some Catholics see it as an opportunity for people to do good, and to learn from.

 pages 216–217

A Complete the table below. First outline the meaning of each characteristic of God. Then explain how each characteristic of God creates the 'problem of evil'.

Characteristics of God	Meaning	How this leads to a problem
Omnipotent		
Omniscient		
Omnibenevolent		

B Complete the boxes around the two categories of evil shown below and on page 76. Explain which category the picture represents, add two examples, then explain why each one creates a problem for Catholics.

Category of evil

_____

_____

Examples

· _____

_____

_____

· _____

_____

Why do they create a problem for Catholics?

_____

_____

_____

_____

_____

_____

Category of evil

_____

_____

Examples

• _____

_____

_____

_____

• _____

_____

_____

_____

_____

Why do they create a problem for Catholics?

_____

_____

_____

_____

_____

_____

_____

_____

_____

c Read the quote below and explain how a Catholic and a non-religious person would interpret this view of God.

‘I form light and create darkness,
I make weal and create woe,
I am the Lord, who do all these things. ’

Isaiah 45:7, RSV-CE

For a Catholic this quote suggests _____

_____

_____

_____

_____

For a non-religious person this quote suggests _____

_____

_____

_____

_____

Activity 4.8: Solutions to the problem of suffering

Potential solutions to the problem of suffering come in three different types: biblical responses, theoretical responses and practical responses.

 pages 218–219

A Sort the following statements about responses to the problem of suffering into the correct categories: biblical, theoretical or practical.

- Prayer is a way to share and respond to suffering.

- St Augustine believed evil was an absence of good and a result of abusing free will.

- God allowed Job to be tested by Satan.

- Helping others is a way to show love to Jesus.

- St Irenaeus believed suffering was the best way to develop and grow.

- Psalm 119 teaches Christians they can learn from their suffering.

- God suffered through Jesus.

Biblical	Theoretical	Practical
• _____	• _____	• _____
_____	_____	_____
_____	_____	_____
• _____	_____	_____
_____	• _____	• _____
_____	_____	_____
_____	_____	_____
• _____	_____	_____
_____	_____	_____

B Now answer the following questions.

1. Which two solutions do you think are the most successful? Explain why you chose them.

1 _____

_____

2 _____

_____

2. Which two solutions do you think are the least successful? Explain why you chose them.

1 _____

_____

2 _____

_____

?/ EXAM PRACTICE

Now answer the following exam question.

(c) Explain **two** ways Catholics believe suffering is something that can be learned from. In your answer you must refer to a source of wisdom and authority. **(5 marks)**

_____

_____

_____

_____

_____

_____

_____

_____

_____

_____

_____

_____

Useful Terms Glossary

As you progress through the course, you can collect the meanings of useful terms in the glossary below. You can then use the completed glossaries to revise from.

To do well in the exam you will need to understand these terms and include them in your answers. Tick the shaded circles to record how confident you feel. Use the extra boxes at the end to record any other terms that you have found difficult, along with their definitions.

○ **I recognise this term**

◔ **I understand what this term means**

● **I can use this term in a sentence**

Miracles _____

Atheist _____

Moral evil _____

Catholic Catechism _____

Natural evil _____

Cosmological argument _____

Omnibenevolent _____

Design argument _____

Omnipotent _____

Humanist _____

Omniscient _____

Philosophical argument

Visions

Religious experience

Revelation

Suffering

St Augustine

St Irenaeus

Chapter 5: **Philosophy and Ethics: Religious Teachings on Relationships and Families in the 21st Century**

Activity 5.1: Catholic ideas on marriage

 **pages 222–224**

Fill in the gaps in the sentences below about marriage using some of the words provided. (There are more words than gaps – you will have to decide which ones to leave out.)

God	charity	civil	sacraments	procreate	ceremony
exclusive	multiply	legal	loving	marks	woman

Catholics believe that _____ instituted marriage from the beginning of

the world when he created man and _____ and told them to 'Be fruitful

and _____' (*Genesis 1:28, RSV-CE*). This is why marriage is one of the seven

_____ of the Catholic Church.

The purposes of marriage can be seen in the _____

or external signs of marriage. Marriage should be seen to be

a _____ relationship and be lifelong. It should

be _____ (only one marriage partner) and fruitful,

giving the opportunity to _____ children.

Couples who are unable to have children can be fruitful in offering

_____ and hospitality. Catholics make promises

about marriage being loving, lifelong, exclusive and fruitful in

the marriage _____.

TIP
You can use the quotation from Genesis 1:28 as a source of wisdom and authority in your exam answers.

Activity 5.2: Divergent views on marriage

These statements giving divergent views on marriage are muddled up.
Write them in the correct places in the table below.

 pages 222–224

- Marriage is only between a man and a woman.

- Cohabitation is acceptable.

- Marriage between same-sex couples is acceptable.

- Marriage is sacred (holy).

- Cohabitation (living together as a couple but not married) is forbidden.

- Civil marriage is an important time to make a public declaration of love and commitment.

Catholic views
• _____
• _____
• _____
_____

Non-religious views
• _____
• _____
• _____
_____

Activity 5.3: Sexual relationships

A Match the correct relationship from the list with the relevant Catholic teaching in the table below.

pages 225–226

Extramarital sex	Same-sex	Cohabitation	Marriage	Premarital sex

	Sexual relations 'bring together a man and woman who are married for the purpose of having children'. Sexual relations should be unitive and procreative. Sexual relations can increase spiritual connection and bring happiness and pleasure.
	This is sex before marriage. The Church teaches that sex is a gift from God to be enjoyed by a married couple – so couples should abstain before marriage.
	This means a couple living together, usually in a sexual relationship, but they are not married.

	This is sex between two men or two women. The Catholic Church teaches that it is not a sin to be homosexual. However, homosexual sex is a sin and homosexuals are expected to remain celibate.
	This is having a sexual relationship with someone while married – breaking the promise to be faithful. It is adultery and is grounds for a civil divorce. However, a Catholic couple would still remain married in the eyes of the Church.

B Complete the following table with Catholic and divergent views on sexual relationships. Some of the sections have been completed for you.

	Catholic Church teaching	Divergent or non-religious views
Sex before marriage and within cohabitation		
Faithfulness in a couple		Most agree that a couple should be faithful following the principle of 'treating others as you would like to be treated'.
Contraception		Thoughtful use of contraception encouraged.
Same-sex relationships		

EXAM PRACTICE

Now answer the following exam question.

(a) Outline **three** non-religious views on sexual relationships. **(3 marks)**

Activity 5.4: The family

Tick the correct answer for each of the questions below.

S B pages 227–229

1. Where do Catholics believe is the most important place for children to learn right from wrong?

☐ School

☐ Family

☐ Friends

☐ Youth clubs

2. Which of the following is **not** a purpose of the family in Catholic teaching?

☐ Lifelong relationships of love and faithfulness.

☐ Support and comfort.

☐ To be a sign of Christ's love in the world.

☐ To encourage people to convert to Catholicism.

3. What does the term 'blended family' refer to?

☐ A single parent bringing up children.

☐ A family led by a same-sex couple.

☐ A family with several generations living together.

☐ Two single-parent families united in a new marriage.

4. Which document reaffirmed Catholic teaching on marriage and the family?

☐ A Humanist Discussion of Family Matters

☐ Synod on the Family 2015

☐ *Familiaris Consortio*

☐ *Humanae Vitae*

SOURCES OF WISDOM AND AUTHORITY

(S B) pages 230–231

Learn this quote from the Catechism of the Catholic Church.

> ❛Parents have the mission of teaching their children to pray and to discover their vocation as children of God.❜
>
> *Catechism of the Catholic Church 2226*

This quote shows the responsibility Catholic parents have to bring their children up in the Catholic faith.

Fill in the gaps below. It will help you to learn the quote if you say the whole thing out loud every time you write it.

❛_____ have the _____ of teaching their children

to _____ and to discover their _____ as children of

_____.❜

Now cover up the text above and have a go at writing out the whole quote from memory.

❛_____

_____

_____❜

B Now answer the following question about this quote.

1. How would attending Mass or taking children along to church groups for children help do this?

_____

_____

_____

_____

Activity 5.5: Support for the family

A Fill in the gaps in the table below about different ways local churches support families.

(SB) pages 230–231

Activity	How these help families
Attending Mass	
F_____ W_____	• Attending Mass together as a family. • There may be a Children's Liturgy providing child-friendly worship and activities.
Classes for parents	
F_____ G_____ M_____	• Parish friendship groups offer monthly meetings for everyone to take part in low-cost activities.
C_____ g_____	• A range of groups for children of different ages including toddler groups, uniformed groups and youth clubs, helping them socialise with other Catholic children and young people.
Counselling and charitable help	
Parish priest or Marriage Care can offer counselling. Natural family planning advice given. Other help such as from charities like St Vincent de Paul	• • •

EXAM PRACTICE

Now answer the following exam question.

(b) Explain **two** ways support from the Church is good for families.

(4 marks)

_____

_____

_____

_____

_____

_____

_____

TIP

Remember that you should write two points and each one should have added detail to gain full marks.

_____

_____

_____

_____

_____

Activity 5.6: Family planning

A Fill in the gaps in the sentences below about different views on family planning using some of the words provided. (There are more words than gaps – you will have to decide which ones to leave out.)

SB pages 232–233

Papal	contraception	everyone	women	abortion	pro-life	procreative
natural	forbidden	decisions	Humanists	fertile	marriage	sex

The Catholic Church teaches that all forms of artificial _____ are wrong.

The Church encourages responsible planning of spacing out the births of children by using the

_____ method of avoiding sex during the more _____

time of a woman's monthly cycle. The Church teaches that contraception undermines the

_____ and unitive nature of a married couple's sexual relationship. This teaching

has been reinforced by the _____ encyclical, *Humanae Vitae*. Catholic teaching

suggests that contraception encourages _____ outside marriage.

Secular _____ generally advise the use of family planning, but unlike Catholic

teaching, recommend that _____, including teenagers, should have access to

contraception. They think this is more likely to mean that every child is a wanted child and result in better

health for _____.

Atheists usually encourage people to make their own _____ about what is

morally right or wrong, including contraception and abortion.

Abortion is specifically _____ by Catholic Church teaching in *Humanae*

Vitae. Secular Humanists and Atheists have traditionally campaigned for a woman's right to have an

_____ if she so chooses.

Activity 5.7: Divorce, annulment and remarriage

SB pages 234–235

A Mark the following statements as true or false.

	True	False
Catholic teaching says that Church (sacramental) marriage is a lifelong commitment.	☐	☐
Annulment means a marriage was never valid.	☐	☐
Catholics are allowed to remarry after a civil divorce.	☐	☐
The Catholic Church does not allow legal separation and divorce.	☐	☐
Some other Christian churches allow remarriage after divorce in some circumstances.	☐	☐
Catholics believe Jesus taught that divorce is acceptable.	☐	☐
Catholics believe that an individual's wishes are more important than the needs of their children.	☐	☐
Situation ethics suggests people should do the most loving thing.	☐	☐

B These statements giving divergent views on divorce, annulment and remarriage are muddled up. Write them in the correct places in the table below.

- Marriage only ends when one of the partners dies or it is annulled.

- Some suggest Jesus allowed divorce when someone had been adulterous, as in Matthew 5:32.

- Christianity is based on forgiveness so people should be allowed a second chance.

- Humanists often support liberal divorce laws recognising that some relationships fail.

- God has joined the man and woman together in marriage.

- Marriage is not 'sacred'.

Catholic teaching on marriage and divorce

- _____

- _____

Other churches' teaching on marriage and divorce

- _____

- _____

Non-religious attitudes to marriage and divorce

- _____

- _____

SOURCES OF WISDOM AND AUTHORITY

SB pages 234–235

A Learn these quotes about divorce.

> ❝I hate divorce, says the Lord the God of Israel.❞
>
> *Malachi 2:16, RSV-CE*

This quote shows that God hates divorce.

Fill in the gaps below. It will help you to learn the quote if you say the whole thing out loud every time you write it.

❝I hate _____, says the Lord the _____ of

_____.❞

Now cover up the text above and have a go at writing out the whole quote from memory.

❝ _____ ❞

> ❝If civil divorce remains the only possible way [...] it can be tolerated and does not constitute a moral offense.❞
>
> *Catechism of the Catholic Church 2283*

This quote shows that in certain circumstances (such as to protect legal rights or to make sure that children are properly cared for) civil divorce is acceptable to the Catholic Church. However, the couple still remain married in the eyes of God.

Fill in the gaps below. It will help you to learn the quote if you say the whole thing out loud every time you write it.

❝If _____ divorce remains the only _____ way [...] it can be

_____ and does not _____ a moral _____.❞

Now cover up the text above and have a go at writing out the whole quote from memory.

❝ _____

_____

_____ ❞

B Now answer the following question about these quotes.

1. How does Catholic teaching on divorce follow the teaching in Malachi 2:16?

_____

_____

_____

EXAM PRACTICE

Now answer the following exam question.

(c) Explain **two** divergent Christian views on divorce. In your answer you must refer to a source of wisdom and authority.

(5 marks)

_____

_____

_____

_____

_____

_____

_____

_____

_____

_____

_____

_____

_____

_____

SOURCES OF WISDOM AND AUTHORITY

SB pages 236–237

A Learn this quote about the equality of men and women.

'So God created man in his own image, in the image of God he created him; male and female he created them.'

Genesis 1:27, RSV-CE

This quote shows that both men and women are made in the image of God, and as such, are equal.

Fill in the gaps below. It will help you to learn the quote if you say the whole thing out loud every time you write it.

'So _____ created man in his own _____, in the image of

God he _____ him; _____ and _____

he created them.'

Now cover up the text above and have a go at writing out the whole quote from memory.

'_____

_____,'

B Now answer the following question about this quote.

1. How does this quote show that men and women are equal in God's sight?

_____

_____

Activity 5.8: Equality of men and women in the family

A Read the following text about equality of men and women within the family.

SB pages 236–237

Adam and Eve are both equally chosen by God and yet both sin, disobeying God. Catechism 2207 emphasises the equality of men and women within the family, as both are responsible for making their marriage work and for looking after children. The emphasis is on partnership. Women are encouraged to have the freedom to go out to work or to be at home caring for their family. Most Christians agree with this, although some still hold more traditional views about the roles of men and women.

There are a variety of views on the roles of men and women in the family in other churches. Some Christians point out that men should be equally supported in managing their home/work life balance. Other Christian groups emphasise the role of the father in earning money and the mother in bringing up the children. Some Christian churches support same-sex couples as they seek to include children in their families. Many churches, both Catholic and non-Catholic, seek to reach out to support families who are experiencing difficulties. This might include single-parent families or families that have become separated, for example refugee families.

B Now answer the following questions.

1. Give two reasons why men and women should be considered equal in marriage.

1 _____

_____

2 _____

_____

2. Explain one difference between the views of the Catholic Church and some other Christian churches on how families should work.

_____

_____

_____

3. Suggest two ways churches might support families experiencing problems.

1 _____

_____

2 _____

_____

4. Think of one practical way a Catholic parish church could support families in difficulty.

_____

_____

_____

Activity 5.9: Gender prejudice and discrimination

 pages 238–239

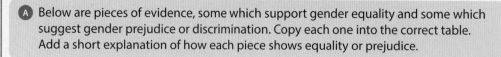 Below are pieces of evidence, some which support gender equality and some which suggest gender prejudice or discrimination. Copy each one into the correct table. Add a short explanation of how each piece shows equality or prejudice.

❝There is … neither male nor female; for you are all one in Christ Jesus.❞

Galatians 3:28, RSV-CE

Jesus treats women with respect in John 4:4–26 (the Samaritan woman at the well) and Matthew 15:21–28 (the Greek woman).

❝Wives be subject to your husbands … For the husband is the head of the wife.❞

Ephesians 5:22–23, RSV-CE

The Church of England has ordained women priests since 1994.

❝Excessive … social disparity between individuals and people of the one human race is a source of scandal.❞

Catechism of the Catholic Church 1938

Some priests left the Church of England and joined the Catholic Church when women were ordained.

❝the women should keep silence in the churches❞

1 Corinthians 14:34, RSV-CE

In *Ordinatio Sacerdotalis* the Catholic Church said that because Jesus did not have female disciples, it could not ordain women as priests.

TIP

Some of these pieces of evidence could be used as sources of wisdom and authority for an exam question on equality.

Evidence which supports gender equality

Evidence: _____

_____

How: _____

_____

Evidence: _____

_____

How: _____

_____

Evidence: _____

_____

How: _____

_____

Evidence: _____

_____

How: _____

_____

Evidence which suggests gender prejudice and discrimination

Evidence: _____

_____

How: _____

_____

Evidence: _____

_____

How: _____

_____

Evidence: _____

_____

How: _____

_____

Evidence: _____

_____

How: _____

_____

🔑 USEFUL TERMS

 pages 234–239

A These terms and their meanings are muddled up. Write out the meanings in the correct order in the second table below.

Gender prejudice	A declaration that a marriage was never valid
Discrimination	A legal separation of the partners in a marriage
Complementary	Believing people of one gender to be better or worse on the basis of their sex
Divorce	Treating a group of people unfairly on the basis of their sex, ethnicity, etc.
Annulment	Men and women are equal but have different strengths and gifts and so can mutually support each other

Gender prejudice	
Discrimination	
Complementary	
Divorce	
Annulment	

B Now write the correct term beside each meaning. For an extra challenge, cover up the rest of this activity and try to see if you can recall the words from memory.

Men and women are equal but have different strengths and gifts and so can mutually support each other	
A legal separation of the partners in a marriage	
A declaration that a marriage was never valid	
Believing people of one gender to be better or worse on the basis of their sex	
Treating a group of people unfairly on the basis of their sex, ethnicity, etc.	

EXAM PRACTICE

Now answer the following exam question.

(d) 'All churches should treat men and women equally.' Evaluate this statement considering arguments for and against. In your response you should:

- refer to Catholic teachings

- refer to different Christian points of view

- reach a justified conclusion. **(12 marks)**

 REMEMBER...

- Focus your answer on the statement you are asked to evaluate.

- Try to write at least three paragraphs – one with arguments to support the statement, one with arguments to support a different point of view, and a final paragraph with a justified conclusion stating which side you think is more convincing, and why.

- Look at the bullet points in the question, and make sure you include everything that they ask for.

- The key skill that you need to demonstrate is **evaluation**. This means expressing judgements on whether an argument is strong or weak, based on evidence. You might decide an argument is strong because it is based on a source of religious wisdom and authority, such as a teaching from the Bible, or because it is based on scientific evidence. You might decide an argument is weak because it is based on a personal opinion, or a popular idea with no scientific basis. You can use phrases such as 'This a convincing argument because…' or 'In my opinion this is a weak argument because…'.

Useful Terms Glossary

As you progress through the course, you can collect the meanings of useful terms in the glossary below. You can then use the completed glossaries to revise from.

To do well in the exam you will need to understand these terms and include them in your answers. Tick the shaded circles to record how confident you feel. Use the extra boxes at the end to record any other terms that you have found difficult, along with their definitions.

○ **I recognise this term**

◐ **I understand what this term means**

● **I can use this term in a sentence**

Divorce

Annulment

Equality

Artificial contraception

Extended family

Blended family

Family planning

Celibate

Gender discrimination

Cohabitation

Gender prejudice

Homosexuality _____

_____

_____

_____

_____

Procreative _____

_____

_____

_____

_____

Marital _____

_____

_____

_____

_____

_____

Remarriage _____

_____

_____

_____

_____

_____

Marriage _____

_____

_____

_____

_____

_____

Sacraments _____

_____

_____

_____

_____

_____

Natural family planning _____

_____

_____

_____

_____

Same-sex family _____

_____

_____

_____

_____

Nuclear family _____

_____

_____

_____

_____

Sanctity _____

_____

_____

_____

_____

Parish _____

_____

_____

_____

_____

_____

Single-parent family _____

_____

_____

_____

_____

_____

Situation ethics

Theology of the body

Unitive

Test the (a) question

Example

1 | Outline **three** examples of religious experience. **(3 marks)**

Mary appearing to Bernadette in Lourdes. ✔ *(1)*

The transfiguration of Jesus as witnessed by Peter, James and John. ✔ *(1)*

The visions of Joan of Arc. ✔ *(1)*

 REMEMBER...

Write your answer as **three sentences**. This will help you to remember that you need to give three pieces of information. Stretch yourself to write three points and don't just repeat yourself – make each point say something new.

WHAT WILL THE QUESTION LOOK LIKE?

The (a) question will always start with the words **'Outline three…'** or **'State three…'**, and a maximum of **3 marks** will be awarded.

HOW IS IT MARKED?

In your answer you should provide three facts or short ideas; **you don't need to explain them or express any opinions**. For each correct response you will receive one mark.

Activity

2 | Outline **three** types of family within 21st-century society. **(3 marks)**

The sample answer below would get only 1 mark, despite the student identifying three types of family. Rewrite the answer to gain 3 marks.

Nuclear. Same-sex. Single-parent. ✔ *(1)*

_____

_____

_____

_____

_____

_____

TIP

Remember, you should write three sentences to answer an 'Outline' question. Sentences start with a capital letter, end with full stop, and need to be two words or more.

3 | Outline **three** teachings of the Catholic Church about sexual relationships. **(3 marks)**

The sample answer below would only gain 1 mark. It contains three separate points but two of them contain factual errors. Identify the two incorrect statements and rewrite them with the correct information.

It may lead to children, if that is the preference of the couple.

It is unitive, bringing together a man and a woman.

TIP

Remember, 'State' questions can come up, although they will be rare. You can answer with just one word for these.

It can take place within marriage, or before it, if you are in love.

_____

_____

_____

_____

_____

4 Outline **three** examples of evil in the world. **(3 marks)**

_____

_____

_____

_____

_____

_____

5 Outline **three** Catholic beliefs about revelation. **(3 marks)**

_____

_____

_____

_____

_____

Test the (b) question

Example

1 | Explain **two** reasons that Catholics believe marriage is important. **(4 marks)**

Firstly, Catholics believe that God instituted marriage as part of Creation. ✔ **(1)**
Adam and Eve were created as the first two humans and told to 'be fruitful and multiply'. ✔ **(1)**

Secondly, Catholics see it as a gift from God and a way of uniting a couple in faithful and mutual love. ✔ **(1)** *This is a reflection of the belief that the two become 'one flesh'.* ✔ **(1)**

> **WHAT WILL THE QUESTION LOOK LIKE?**
>
> The (b) question will always start with the words **'Explain two…'** or **'Describe two…'**, and a maximum of **4 marks** will be awarded. You are asked to 'Explain' or 'Describe', which means you will need to show **development** of ideas.

> **HOW IS IT MARKED?**
>
> This answer would gain 4 marks because it makes two different points, and both points are clearly developed.

> **!** **REMEMBER…**
>
> Make **two different points**. Try to show the examiner where each point begins. For example, start your answer with 'Firstly…' and then move on to your second point by saying 'Secondly…'.
>
> Try to **develop** each point with an example or more explanation. Developing your points will earn you more marks.

Activity

2 | Explain **two** solutions to the problem of suffering for Catholics. **(4 marks)**

The sample answer below would get 2 out of 4 marks as neither point is developed. Develop each point fully for a maximum of 2 additional marks.

One solution is to remember Jesus suffered too. ✔ **(1)**

_____

_____

_____

A second solution is to give to charity. ✔ **(1)**

_____

_____

_____

> **TIP**
>
> Remember that to develop a point you need to give an example or more explanation. Phrases such as 'This means that…', 'This is where…', or 'For example…' can be a good way to start developing a point.

3 Explain **two** ways that a parish may offer support to families. **(4 marks)**

The sample answer below would get 2 marks because it makes one point and then develops it with more explanation. Add a second point for 1 more mark. If you can develop that point with an appropriate example or more explanation, you will get the total 4 marks available.

Firstly, there are often catechesis programmes for parents as part of the preparation for the sacraments such as baptism or first Holy Communion. ✔ **(1)** It is not only the children who receive input, but also the parents to help them understand Catholic teaching better. ✔ **(1)**

Secondly... _____

_____

_____

_____

4 Explain **two** ways in which visions could be proof of the existence of God. **(4 marks)**

The sample answer below has begun two points. Complete and develop each one.

The first reason is that there are many examples in the Bible _____

_____

_____

_____

The second reason is that they can be powerful, personal experiences _____

_____

_____

_____

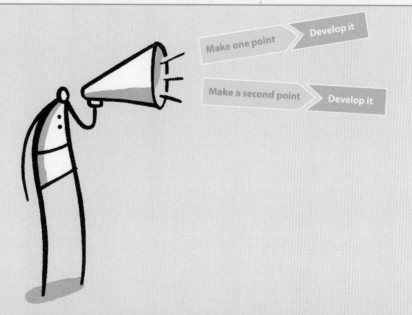

Make one point → Develop it

Make a second point → Develop it

5 Explain **two** reasons why the Catholic Church does not allow divorce.　　　**(4 marks)**

6 Explain **two** things the revelation of Jesus shows about the nature of God.　　　**(4 marks)**

Test the (c) question

Example

WHAT WILL THE QUESTION LOOK LIKE?

The (c) question will always start with the words **'Explain two…'** and end with the words **'In your answer you must refer to a source of wisdom and authority'**. A maximum of **5 marks** will be awarded.

1 | Explain **two** reasons why miracles may lead to belief in God. In your answer you must refer to a source of wisdom and authority. **(5 marks)**

Firstly, many Christians believe that miracles are one way God communicates with humans to reveal his omnipotent nature, which leads to their belief in him. ✓ **(1)** *This is because miracles are events that cannot be explained by science.* ✓ **(1)**

Secondly, there is a biblical tradition of miracles leading to belief, ✓ **(1)** *which continues to inspire Christians today. It was clear that God intervened in the lives of early Christians as he seemingly continues to do today.* ✓ **(1)** *For example, Jesus healed an official's son without even seeing him and this made the man believe Jesus' word.* ✓ **(1)** *Therefore miracles today may also lead to belief in God.*

HOW IS IT MARKED?

This answer would gain 5 marks because it makes two different points, and both points are clearly developed. It also refers to a relevant source of wisdom and authority.

REMEMBER…

The 5 mark question is similar to the 4 mark question, so try to make **two different points** and **develop** each of them.

The additional instruction in the question asks you to **'refer to a source of wisdom and authority'**. Try to think of a reference to the Bible, the Catechism, the words of a prayer or a quote from a saint, pope or bishop that can back up one of your points. You only need one reference.

Activity

2 | Explain **two** reasons why natural family planning can help Catholics be more faithful Christians. In your answer you must refer to a source of wisdom and authority. **(5 marks)**

Write the following points into an exam-style answer for the question above (there are more writing lines on the next page).

Simple	Developed	Source of wisdom and authority
It does not separate the unitive and procreative nature of sexual relationships.	Even though it is near impossible for the woman to get pregnant, there is not an artificial barrier stopping the procreative nature, which is strictly forbidden.	
Only natural family planning is permitted, therefore to be faithful, it is this that needs to be followed.	This is because artificial contraception is seen as contradicting the will of God, despite it being more popular in society.	This is made clear in 'Humanae Vitae' written by Paul VI.

_____

_____

_____

_____

_____

_____

3 Explain **two** things the Design Argument shows about the nature of God for Catholics. In your answer you must refer to a source of wisdom and authority. **(5 marks)**

The key source of wisdom and authority here is 'Ever since the creation of the world his invisible nature, namely his eternal power and deity, has been clearly perceived in the things that have been made.' (*Romans 1:20, RSV-CE*).

The sample answer below has begun two points connected to this quote, each gaining 1 mark. Develop both points and add a part of the quote to support the first point you make.

The first thing it shows is God's omnipotence. ✔ **(1)** Only God would have the power to _____

_____

_____

_____

This is made clear in Romans when it says, '_____

_____

The second thing it shows is God's omniscience. ✔ **(1)** The world is so complex and intricate

_____

_____

_____

4 Explain **two** reasons why Catholics would campaign against gender prejudice. In your answer you must refer to a source of wisdom and authority. **(5 marks)**

Use the following quote to support one of your two developed points: 'disparity between individuals and people of the one human race is a source of scandal' (*CCC 1938*).

TIP

Remember that you only need to refer to one source of wisdom and authority. This can be linked to either your first point or your second point.

_____
_____
_____
_____
_____
_____
_____
_____
_____

5 Explain **two** reasons why God can still be seen as all loving despite suffering in the world. In your answer you must refer to a source of wisdom and authority. **(5 marks)**

_____
_____
_____
_____
_____
_____
_____
_____
_____

Test the (d) question

Example

1 'There is always a solution to suffering for Catholics.'

Evaluate this statement considering arguments for and against. In your response you should:

- refer to Catholic teachings
- reach a justified conclusion.   **(15 marks)**

In this question, 3 of the marks awarded will be for your spelling, punctuation and grammar and your use of specialist terminology.

WHAT WILL THE QUESTION LOOK LIKE?

The (d) question will always ask you to **evaluate** a statement. The bullet points underneath will tell you the things the examiner expects to see in your answer. Here, it says you need to 'refer to Catholic teachings', so make sure you write about core Catholic beliefs, or important sources of Catholic wisdom and authority. The final bullet will always ask you to 'reach a justified conclusion'.

SPaG

On Paper 3A, you will be assessed on the quality of your written communication in questions 1 (d) – relating to Arguments for the Existence of God. A maximum of 3 marks will be awarded for consistent accuracy in your **spelling, punctuation and grammar**, and for using a wide range of specialist terms. Allow yourself time in the exam to check this (d) answer carefully.

(!) REMEMBER...

To evaluate the statement, you need to:
- explain why some people might agree with the statement
- give reasons, including Catholic views
- say whether you think this is a strong or weak argument, and explain why.

Then:
- explain why other people might disagree with the statement
- give reasons, including Catholic views
- say whether you think this is a strong or weak argument, and explain why.

What might make a strong argument?
- Based on a religious source of wisdom and authority, for example a teaching from the Bible or the Catechism, or from the Pope.
- Based on scientific evidence.

What might make a weak argument?
- Based on personal opinion rather than a religious teaching.
- A popular idea with no scientific basis.

Reaching a justified conclusion means you need to:
- explain which side of the argument you think has the strongest evidence
- refer to this evidence briefly.

HOW IS IT MARKED?

The examiner will mark your answer using a mark scheme based on level descriptors, similar to the ones below.

Level descriptors

Level 1 (1–3 marks)	• Basic information or issues related to the topic are loosely identified and can be explained with limited religious or moral understanding.
	• Judgements are given but not fully explained or justified.
Level 2 (4–6 marks)	• Some information or issues related to the topic are identified and can be explained with religious or moral understanding.
	• Judgements are given with some attempt to appraise the evidence, but they are not fully explained or justified.
Level 3 (7–9 marks)	• Information given clearly describes religious information/issues, leading to coherent and logical chains of reasoning that consider different viewpoints. These are supported by an accurate understanding of religion and belief.
	• The answer contains coherent and reasoned judgements of many, but not all, of the elements in the question. Judgements are supported by a good understanding of evidence, leading to a partially justified conclusion.

Level 4 (10–12 marks)	• The response critically deconstructs religious information/issues, leading to coherent and logical chains of reasoning that consider different viewpoints. These are supported by a sustained, accurate and thorough understanding of religion and belief.
	• The answer contains coherent and reasoned judgements of the full range of elements in the question. Judgements are fully supported by the comprehensive use of evidence, leading to a fully justified conclusion.

Here are four sample answers to the question on the previous page. Each one would be awarded a different level. Read through the answers to get an idea of what a level 1, 2, 3 or 4 answer looks like.

Level 1 sample answer:

This is a Level 1 answer because:
• it only gives brief reasons to support one side of the argument
• there is very little evaluation of the arguments.

To improve this answer the student should:
• include the other side of the argument plus reasons to support it
• explain whether they think the arguments are strong or weak.

Despite the huge amount of suffering in the world, Catholics can find a way to deal with it by looking to the Bible. They can read about Jesus suffering, and Job in the Old Testament. These will bring comfort. Catholics can also look at ways to respond, perhaps by prayer or by charity. They will want to make a difference. Therefore, I agree as this makes it clear that there is always a solution to suffering.

> **TIP**
> There are some good reasons in support of the statement here. However, the question requires you to evaluate arguments for and against.

Level 2 sample answer:

This is a Level 2 answer because:
• it refers to different arguments linked to the statement
• it comes to a conclusion about which side is correct.

To improve this answer the student should:
• evaluate how strong or weak each of the arguments is
• explain why they think the arguments are strong or weak.

The Bible provides a solution to suffering for Catholics; they can be comforted by the stories contained in both the Old and New Testaments. For example, Job is a good man who God allows to be tormented by Satan showing humans don't always understand suffering. Also, Jesus demonstrates that God suffered too.

Catholics can also look at ways to respond, perhaps by prayer or by charity. These are practical solutions for Catholics where they will try to communicate with God, and then they might do something like give money to a good cause after this. This will make them realise they are making a difference.

However on the other hand, many people do lose their faith due to the amount of evil and suffering in the world. David Hume called the problem of evil, the 'rock of atheism'. It shows that there is not always a solution to suffering.

In conclusion, it is clear that there is not always a solution, yet most Catholics do find a response in the Bible or from practical solutions. Therefore it's impossible to fully agree with the statement, but most Catholics do find some kind of solution.

> **TIP**
> Starting a paragraph with 'However...' is a good way to signpost the start of a second view.

> **TIP**
> It is acceptable to partly agree with a statement if you can explain why. A vague statement such as 'there are strengths and weaknesses for both' would not be a real conclusion. Here however the student has expressed a judgement and given a reason for why they have reached that judgement.

Level 3 sample answer:

This is a Level 3 answer because:
- it evaluates arguments on both sides
- it comes to a conclusion based on this evaluation.

To improve this answer the student should:
- give some more evidence on each side to strengthen the arguments
- evaluate this evidence.

The Bible provides a convincing solution to suffering for many Catholics; they can be comforted by the stories contained in both the Old and New Testaments. For example, Job is a good man who God allows to be tormented by Satan showing humans don't always understand suffering. Also, Jesus demonstrates that God suffered too – and that there can be a purpose to it. These are strong reasons as Catholics feel these solutions could relate to them.

Catholics can also look at ways to respond, perhaps by prayer or by charity. These practical solutions are often helpful and convincing solutions for Catholics where they will share and seek comfort by communicating with God, often followed by action or donation. This will make them realise they are making a difference, and therefore is a strong reason.

However on the other hand, many people do lose their faith due to the amount of evil and suffering in the world. David Hume called the problem of evil, the 'rock of atheism'. It shows that there is not always a solution to suffering. The fact that significant numbers of people have doubted or even lost their faith shows the strength of this reason. Additionally, natural evil cannot be seen as a misuse of free will, and many people do not find it convincing to explain natural disasters as having an unknown purpose.

In conclusion, it is clear that there is not always a solution, yet most Catholics do find a response in the Bible or from practical solutions. Therefore it's impossible to fully agree with the statement, but most Catholics do find some kind of solution as they find the Bible, theoretical responses such as Augustine's theodicy or practical responses as convincing.

TIP

To reach Level 3 you should evaluate the arguments for each side. Don't just wait until you get to the conclusion. Using phrases such as 'The fact that... shows...' is a good way to show that you are evaluating.

TIP

Make sure you write a justified conclusion, rather than just giving your personal opinion. This conclusion is 'justified' because it refers to the evidence that has led the student to agree with the statement.

Level 4 sample answer:

This is a Level 4 answer because:
- there is a clear line of argument throughout
- it evaluates the arguments it presents and leads to a clear conclusion
- there is evidence the student knows a lot about the topic, and the whole answer is clearly linked to the statement.

The Bible provides a very convincing solution to suffering for many Catholics; they can be comforted by the stories contained in both the Old and New Testaments. For example, Job is a good man who God allows to be tormented by Satan, showing humans don't always understand suffering. Also, Jesus demonstrates that God suffered too – and that there can be a purpose to it. These are strong reasons for Catholics which are hard to overcome, especially knowing that Jesus suffered too.

Catholics can also look at ways to respond, perhaps by prayer or by charity. These practical solutions are often helpful and convincing solutions for Catholics where they will share and seek comfort by communicating with God, often followed by action or donation. This supplements their reflections upon scripture, and ensures they act in a loving and compassionate way to those who are suffering and is therefore is a strong reason.

On the other hand, many people do lose their faith due to the amount of evil and suffering in the world. David Hume called the problem of evil, the 'rock of atheism'. It shows that there is not always a solution to suffering. The fact that significant numbers of people have doubted or even lost their faith shows the strength of this reason. Additionally, natural evil cannot be seen as a misuse of free will, and many people do not find it convincing to explain natural disasters as having an unknown purpose. For some these reasons do carry more weight than any response or scriptural justification, especially if they have been personally affected.

In conclusion, it is clear that there is not always a solution, yet most Catholics do find a response in the Bible or from practical solutions. Therefore it's impossible to fully agree with the statement, but most Catholics do find some kind of solution as they find the Bible, theoretical responses such as Augustine's theodicy or practical responses as convincing.

TIP
You need to use logical chains of reasoning in your answers. In this first paragraph the student has made a point, given a reason, used an example to explain that reason and come to a conclusion which links everything they have said together.

TIP
Accurate sources of wisdom and authority can be useful for providing evidence to back up your arguments in the (d) question.

TIP
Don't forget that 3 marks are given for accurate spelling, punctuation and grammar and the use of specialist terminology. Vocabulary such as 'scriptural justification', 'theoretical responses' and 'theodicy' show this student can express their arguments using the correct terms.

TIP
This is a very well-structured response with a clear line of argument. It is always worthwhile spending a few minutes to plan your response. Start by thinking of arguments for and against the statement. Think of the evidence you will use to back up each side and remember to comment on how convincing you think the arguments are, and why.

Remember to end with a justified conclusion, stating which side you find more convincing, and explaining why you think this.

Activity

2 'A Catholic can never get divorced.'

Evaluate this statement considering arguments for and against. In your response you should:

- refer to Catholic teachings
- reach a justified conclusion. **(12 marks)**

A Read the sample answer below.

The Catholic teaching on the sacrament of Holy Matrimony is very clear as the four marks are: loving, lifelong, exclusive and fruitful. It is obvious that if a marriage is lifelong, it cannot be ended with divorce. This is a strong reason for Catholics not accepting divorce; they believe marriage is a covenant that cannot be dissolved because God has joined the man and woman together (CCC 2382).

Furthermore, Jesus was very firm that divorce was wrong, and that it only happened due to people refusing to obey God's law. In the Old Testament, it is said that 'God hates divorce'. This is a very convincing reason for agreeing with the statement.

For Catholics, the teaching is very clear. The covenant of marriage can only end through death or annulment, which is very rare. Therefore the arguments are very strong and convincing for divorce not being possible for Catholics.

However, it is important to understand that a Catholic may seek a civil divorce and separation. This can happen for the safety or health of the couple or children. This suggests then that a Catholic can get divorced, but does not mean the sacrament has ended, nor can they get remarried.

Additionally, a civil divorce is required for an annulment, therefore the Church would insist on a divorce taking place, which goes against the claim made in the statement that Catholics can never get divorced.

In conclusion, it is clear that in order to fully answer this, a distinction needs to be made between sacramental and civil divorce. For Catholics, a sacramental divorce is simply not possible, as what has been joined in matrimony by God, cannot be separated by earthly power. However, a legal divorce is possible and even required in some cases. Assuming Catholics are talking about a sacramental divorce, the statement is clearly correct, as it is just not possible.

B Now answer the following questions about the sample answer above.

1. The student makes several arguments to support the statement. Explain two of them.

_____

_____

_____

2. Do you agree that these are strong arguments? Why or why not?

_____

_____

_____

3. The student gives an argument against the statement. What is it?

_____

_____

_____

4. Why does the student suggest this argument is not the same as the ones in support of the statement?

_____

_____

_____

5. Do you agree with the student's conclusion? Why or why not?

_____

_____

_____

6. The question says you should 'refer to Catholic teachings'. Using a coloured pen, highlight any references to Catholic teaching that you can find.

7. The question also asks you to 'reach a justified conclusion'. Circle the sentence where the student gives their judgement. Then underline the sentence where they summarise their evidence.

8. Can you find and highlight any phrases which show that the student is evaluating the arguments?

TIP

Remember, evaluating means making a judgement about how strong or weak an argument is, based on evidence.

3 'The Design Argument convinces Catholics of God's existence.'

Evaluate this statement considering arguments for and against. In your response you should:

• refer to Catholic teachings

• refer to non-religious points of view

• reach a justified conclusion. **(15 marks)**

In this question, 3 of the marks awarded will be for your spelling, punctuation and grammar and your use of specialist terminology.

Here is the beginning of a response to the question above, which gives some arguments in support of the statement. To complete the answer you need to give arguments against the statement and a justified conclusion.

To move above Level 2 you also need to include judgements, evaluating how convincing you find the arguments to be.

Complete the answer below.

• Begin your first paragraph with the sentence, 'However some Catholics would disagree with these ideas because…'.

• Include arguments from the non-religious point of view which may support or oppose your arguments.

• Include some evaluation, such as 'This argument is strong/weak because…'.

• Finally, add a justified conclusion. This could begin, 'After considering both sides of the argument, the most convincing reason is…'.

The Teleological or Design Argument presents a very convincing case for many Catholics. The book of Romans makes it clear that God has been seen in creation from the very beginning, and this was fully explained by the great Catholic thinker St Thomas Aquinas and his Fve ways. These are strong arguments that have stood the test of time.

The idea of God as designer is strong and convincing as it is based on the experience of humans – there appears to be design, purpose and order in our world that everyone can observe. Additionally, it complements the Christian view of God, giving a complete explanation of the universe. Finally, it encourages scientific examination of the universe – if you believe there to be order, you want to study it, and this is the very nature of science.

4 'The parish is the best support for families.'

Evaluate this statement considering arguments for and against. In your response you should:

- refer to Catholic teachings
- reach a justified conclusion. **(12 marks)**

 REMEMBER...

- Focus your answer on the statement you are asked to evaluate.

- Try to write at least three paragraphs – one with arguments to support the statement, one with arguments to support a different point of view, and a final paragraph with a justified conclusion stating which side you think is more convincing, and why.

- Look at the bullet points in the question, and make sure you include everything that they ask for.

- The key skill that you need to demonstrate is **evaluation**. This means expressing judgements on whether an argument is strong or weak, based on evidence. You might decide an argument is strong because it is based on a source of religious wisdom and authority, such as a teaching from the Bible, or because it is based on scientific evidence. You might decide an argument is weak because it is based on a personal opinion, or a popular idea with no scientific basis. You can use phrases such as 'This a convincing argument because…' or 'In my opinion this is a weak argument because…'.

5 'Non-religious arguments about religious experiences are easily overcome.'

Evaluate this statement considering arguments for and against. In your response you should:

- refer to Catholic teachings
- refer to non-religious points of view
- reach a justified conclusion. **(15 marks)**

In this question, 3 of the marks awarded will be for your spelling, punctuation and grammar and your use of specialist terminology.

OXFORD
UNIVERSITY PRESS

Great Clarendon Street, Oxford, OX2 6DP, United Kingdom

Oxford University Press is a department of the University of Oxford.
It furthers the University's objective of excellence in research,
scholarship, and education by publishing worldwide. Oxford is a
registered trade mark of Oxford University Press in the UK and in
certain other countries

© Oxford University Press 2019

The moral rights of the authors have been asserted

First published in 2019

British Library Cataloguing in Publication Data
Data available

978-0-19-844495-4

1 3 5 7 9 10 8 6 4 2

Paper used in the production of this book is a natural, recyclable
product made from wood grown in sustainable forests.
The manufacturing process conforms to the environmental
regulations of the country of origin.

Printed in India by Manipal Technologies Limited

Acknowledgements
We are grateful to the authors and publishers for use of extracts
from their titles and in particular for the following:

Excerpts from **The Stone Edition of the Tanach** (Mesorah
Publications, 2010). © ArtScroll / Mesorah Publications, Ltd.
Reproduced with permission from ArtScroll / Mesorah
Publications, Ltd.

Scripture quotations taken from **The Revised Standard Version
of the Bible: Catholic Edition**, copyright © 1965, 1966 the
Division of Christian Education of the National Council of the
Churches of Christ in the United States of America. Used by
permission. All rights reserved.

Excerpts from **Catechism of the Catholic Church**, http://
www.vatican.va/archive/ccc_css/archive/catechism/ccc_toc.htm
(Strathfield, NSW: St Pauls, 2000). © Libreria Editrice Vaticana.
Reproduced with permission from The Vatican.

Cover photo: Baloncici/iStockphoto

Illustrations: Jason Ramasami and Q2A Media Services Pvt. Ltd

Photos: p9: Moses (Approaching Mt. Sinai), 1905–07 (oil on
canvas), Ury, Lesser (1861–1931) / Tel Aviv Museum of Art, Israel
/ Gift of Georg Kareski / Bridgeman Images; **p32**: ASAP / Alamy
Stock Photo; **p64**: CountrySideCollection – Homer Sykes / Alamy
Stock Photo; **p67**: JOHN KELLERMAN / Alamy Stock Photo; **p72(T)**:
Volodymyr Burdiak / Shutterstock; **p72(B)**: photobyphotoboy /
Shutterstock; **p73**: patrimonio designs ltd / Shutterstock; **p81**:
Rawpixel Ltd / Alamy Stock Photo.

Please note that the practice questions in this book allow students
a genuine attempt at practising exam skills, but they are not
intended to replicate examination papers.

Thank you
OUP wishes to thank Julie Haigh, Rabbi Benjy Rickman and Mark
Shepstone for their help reviewing this book.